WALKING THROUGH MADNESS

EMILY KNEW

FriesenPress

Suite 300 - 990 Fort St
Victoria, BC, V8V 3K2
Canada

www.friesenpress.com

Copyright © 2019 by Emily Knew
First Edition — 2019

All rights reserved.

No part of this publication may be reproduced in any form, or by any means, electronic or mechanical, including photocopying, recording, or any information browsing, storage, or retrieval system, without permission in writing from FriesenPress.

ISBN
978-1-5255-5174-1 (Hardcover)
978-1-5255-5175-8 (Paperback)
978-1-5255-5176-5 (eBook)

1. BIOGRAPHY & AUTOBIOGRAPHY, PERSONAL MEMOIRS

Distributed to the trade by The Ingram Book Company

Thank you!

I wanted to give a special thank you to Laura Matheson. You are a dynamite editor that has been perfect for me. Thank you for your kindness. I can feel that you get it and understand, and that has made this a truly wonderful experience for me.

Emily the child within Dillon

"There is something wrong with Emily," I overheard my mother telling her friend while they drank coffee.

My mind was racing and I didn't understand why my mother was saying this. My head dropped and a fear welled up deep inside me. *Mom knows I'm not far away, so why is she saying this?* A sick feeling overcame my stomach. I couldn't move and wondered what was wrong with me.

My chest tightened and tears wanted to roll from my eyes. *How will I be able to conceal how afraid I am?*

Why was my mother saying this about me? *Why?*

I did know, sadly.

I did know why she was saying this …

I wasn't like the other kids, but why?

TABLE OF CONTENTS

Chapter 1: My First Birthday Party 1

Chapter 2: Grade One 5

Chapter 3: The Strange Doctor 9

Chapter 4: Sunday Sports 11

Chapter 5: Elementary School 13

Chapter 6: Crushing Nightmares 17

Chapter 7: Okanagan Fruit 19

Chapter 8: No Roughhousing 23

Chapter 9: The Bad House 25

Chapter 10: More Nightmares 29

Chapter 11: The Poem 31

Chapter 12: Ironing 33

Chapter 13: Dad & Mom 35

Chapter 14: Skeletons in the Closet 41

Chapter 15: Secrets & Hiding Places 45

Chapter 16: Locked Doors 47

Chapter 17: Clothes Make the Woman 49

Chapter 18: Hot Dog Day 51

Chapter 19: Cleaning and the Laundry Chute 53
Chapter 20: The Fighter 59
Chapter 21: Growing Strong 63
Chapter 21 Alone 65
Chapter 22: It Is What It Is 69
Chapter 23: Babysitting 73
Chapter 25: The Door 75
Chapter 26: Winter 77
Chapter 27: Party? What Party? 79
Chapter 28: When Christmas Changed 81
Chapter 29: High School 83
Chapter 30: Excellent Hiding Spots 87
Chapter 31: Long Weekend 89
Chapter 32: What is wrong with her? 93
Chapter 33: Nancy's Boyfriend 95
Chapter 34: Toys 97
Chapter 35: She's a Very Wilful Girl 99
Chapter 36: Life Changes 103
Chapter 37: Marriage and Babies 105
Chapter 38: I Was Lost 109
Chapter 39: Nightmares, Secrets, and Locked Doors 113
Chapter 40: Mom's Blue Dress 119
Chapter 41: I Have Questions 123
Chapter 42: Flash Way Back! 127
Chapter 43: Nancy's Memories 129
Chapter 44: Our Cherry Tree Grandparents 135

Chapter 45: Balloons! Why? 137
Chapter 46: The Questions Pile Up 141
Chapter 47: Games Others Play with Our Hearts 143
Chapter 48: What Would Normal People Do? 149
Chapter 49: Love Me, Love Me Not 155
Chapter 50: Making Christmas Memories 159
Chapter 51: Strange Things 163
Chapter 52: Who is This Woman? 167
Chapter 53: Learning to be Afraid 173
Chapter 54: Left Behind 175
Chapter 55: The Summer Everything Changed 177
Chapter 56: That Was It 181
Chapter 57: You're going to Scare the Other Kids 183
Chapter 58: A Strange Question 185
Chapter 59: The Puzzle Takes Shape 191
Chapter 60: The Memories Just Don't Stop 193
Chapter 61: Stop! 197
Chapter 62: Some People Are Just Born Slow… 201
Chapter 63: Feel My Skull 205
Chapter 64: I Had to Know 209
Chapter 65: The Picture 211
Chapter 66: Something inside Me Broke 213
Chapter 67: A Flooding Mind 215
Chapter 68: What is Love? 219
Chapter 69: I Had a Dream, Years Ago 223
Chapter 70: A Mystery 225

CHAPTER 1: MY FIRST BIRTHDAY PARTY

I heard my mom calling me. I was in my bedroom. She was telling me I was going to be late for a birthday party. I didn't know there was a party and had no idea I was invited. It was for Jeannette, my friend from kindergarten. I didn't have a good memory what was wrong with me. "Go put on a dress and hurry we're going to be late." Mom was calling. I always forgot things. There *was* something wrong with me and I knew it.

"You know I don't have a driver licence and I shouldn't even be driving. Oh, I hope we'll be okay. Listen, you behave at this party." Mom worried a lot when she was driving because she knew that she shouldn't be driving. What if the police stopped her with no driver's licence? I felt very nervous and excited, wondering what was going to happen at this party.

I really liked Jeannette because she was nice to me and she was very pretty with her big, soft brown eyes. When we pulled up to

Jeanette's house, I remember taking it all in. My eyes full of wonderment, I noticed the lawn was cut and the flowers in the front yard were beautiful. Mom got out of the car, took hold of my hand, and headed for the front door. I had never been inside Jeanette's home and I didn't realize there would be so many children there. They were running about the house. I was looking forward to seeing Jeannette again. She liked me even though I wasn't smart like the other kids from kindergarten, and from the looks of it, they were all here.

The door was open, but I just stood and stared. I don't even know if I was breathing. My mind went happily blank. The house was so noisy and kids were running around. My eyes were drinking it all in. Kids were laughing and playing. They had music on and balloons of all different colours floated in the air. The table was piled with birthday presents atop a pretty tablecloth with lace around the edges. I don't think I moved, as I was just amazed, frozen like a statue, standing outside the door. All I could think was that these other kids weren't behaving, but Mom suddenly jerked my hand to make me wake up and move and we went inside. I let go of Mom's hand and I found Jeannette and said hi. I was so glad to see her, but she had so many friend in the house. She dashed off, chasing balloons with the other kids. I remember wondering if my mother would leave so I could play like the other kids. {She did not. I could see that she was talking with Jeannette's mom in the kitchen and watching me.} I don't remember how long into this party it was, but I found myself sitting in Jeannette's bedroom alone, looking at this clock she had her bedroom. Her room was beautiful. The walls were painted pink, just like her bedspread, with flowers and ruffles. I was thinking it was like a fairy tale. She was a lucky girl. Click.

The numbers on this clock were red and would flip over for a new number. I had never seen this before. I was sitting in her bedroom alone because I didn't know anything that these kids were doing or how to join in because they were making so much noise. To me these kids should be in trouble, running around the house like they were. I found all this to be just too much and too fast for me to handle. So there I sat, alone, watching the clock's numbers change. Click, it made a *click* sound.

Mom, who was watching me, made excuses to Jeanette's mom. "Emily isn't feeling well." Some said goodbye and Mom took me back home early. I was sad, but I didn't fight it because I knew better and knew to do as I was told. I didn't know why I felt so lost and confused. The other kids ran so fast and were laughing and it did look like fun, like outside at kindergarten. I, for some reason, couldn't join in; it really was too fast, all that running and the music. Plus, having my mom there watching made me know I'd better behave. I think both of these were at play.

I thought about this for a very long time, the whole party stuff. I really was puzzled about this event. Why were these kids able to run about the house and not get into trouble? I had never seen anything like this, so this birthday party I thought must only be for rich kids. I didn't see the gifts being opened or the birthday cake or any of the party games. I was not sure what it was with me, but I was so very different from all my new friends, and I could not help but wonder why. I knew better than to ask any questions because Mom didn't like it if you did. She would get mad. I struggled to understand because things were not like what those kids were up to. Running around the house when your parents were around? Unheard of.

Questioning myself, I felt so very sad and very much rejected. I remembered this birthday party for a long time in my mind and my heart. It did look like fun. My mom had told a neighbour lady while I was sitting in the next room that something was not right with me and she was not lying; there was something wrong with me. I am aware of it because my new friends didn't struggle with new words like I did and I sure didn't remember things like these other kids either. Mom had told me that I almost failed kindergarten. I really didn't understand what that meant, but I did know it wasn't good by the way Mom said it in a flat tone of voice. I lacked the basic concept of understanding.

CHAPTER 2: GRADE ONE

I was happy about going to a new school for grade one because I wouldn't have to take the bus. It was closer to our home, and I could walk the four blocks by myself. I didn't know what to expect, but when I got there I found lots of other kids around, and that was great. Mom came with me on the first day and then would have to leave. I have got to say it was thrilling. I was with all these other kids, and a lady called a teacher. I couldn't wait to start talking and playing, sitting at my desk, thinking how wonderful this was. The school was a much bigger building to explore. I wondered why these other kids knew so much—lots of things—and my questions started off at full speed.

I soon knew some kids didn't like me because I asked so many questions, but other kids thought I was funny, and I was lucky enough to have some kids who would play with me. I discovered humour worked pretty good for me. So I did my best to stay funny. I really enjoyed going to school and being with the other children. We had to sit at our desk in class, and this was better than the birthday party at Jeannette's because we weren't all running around and there was no music playing, just the voice of our teacher.

School, however, did not like me very much because I was just was not getting it. I just could not remember things. I was afraid to put my hand up and even more horrified if the teacher asked me if I knew the answer because I didn't know the answers. The other kids would laugh at me when I didn't know the answers. I was still struggling to just say these new words. I looked at the other kids, and it all seemed easy for them, but I just felt lost. Heck, I could hardly sit still, looking out the windows watching birds fly by. All I wanted to do was go outside and play. Waiting for recess to come seemed to take forever.

Parent-teacher meetings came, and I thought this would be fun because my mom could meet my new teacher. Dad didn't come because of work, so I happily went with my mom, so I could show her my desk. But when the teacher started to talk about me I was to leave and wait outside the door. When Mom came out she was not happy with me and said that I was not understanding the things that were being taught in class. I knew that I was in trouble. I felt sick and wanted to cry because it was true I was not smart like the other kids. I just couldn't remember things; even colouring the pretty pictures was a challenge for me, so I would copy and colour the same as the others.

Mom told me if I didn't get better that I might fail. I really didn't understand because I was trying as hard as I could, and I had no clue how to help myself get better. Later, I overheard Mom tell Dad that those teachers didn't know how to teach me because I was smart enough to play card games. This made me feel better as I really wanted to try to do better, but it would seem that my head was empty. I guess the material was just too difficult for me. Mom pushed the teacher, and I passed grade one. I sure didn't like the feeling of being a failure, and the other kids were seeing that I wasn't smart, but I didn't know what I could do about it.

My brother and sister heard our parents talking about there being something wrong with me, so they would tease me about being a dummy. I can remember listening to Dad and Mom talking about how stupid I was, but I was a girl, so school wasn't all that important for me anyway. Remembering Mom's words about the teachers not knowing how to teach me did make me feel closer to my mom. She was standing up for me because I can play cards.

Mom was also told by the teacher that she would have to work with me if I was going to catch up. Mom didn't like helping me. I remember sitting at the kitchen table, looking at the papers in front of me. Mom was getting mad because I didn't know what I was to do. I cried, worrying because nothing made any sense. The more I worried, the more empty my head was, and the madder Mom got. Mom would walk up to me and say, "Well, are you done yet? Because you can't leave the table until you're done."

She didn't really help. It was like in school. I just don't understand, so again I was alone, trying to understand the non-understandable. It was so frustrating. When Mom looked over at me, she said, "Homework makes me unhappy, and you are happier if I just don't help you." Mom said that I would be okay, and I liked that Mom wanted me to be happy, so she just let me go and do whatever I wanted, and I was gone like a shot.

As for those parent-teacher meetings all through my school years, Mom just stopped going to them as much as she could because she was too busy going out with Dad. I don't think Dad came to any of them. I can remember other kids cleaning up their desks for when their parents came to see how they were doing. I knew that my parents wouldn't be coming, so I made jokes about not having anyone coming to look in at what I was doing with my friends. I would go to the school on the nights of parent-teacher meeting because some of my friends were there and we'd just hang out. I thought things were pretty good because I didn't have anyone telling me what to do. I could make the three blocks home without ever touching the roadways. I went through the trees in the slight dark sky, and I could hide anywhere.

However, the teachers must have asked to see my parents because once in a while, Mom would show up in her beautiful dress for a very fast stop by. She was always too busy to really have a talk with them. School had turned into an awful place to go, and I had fewer friends; the difference between my friends and myself seemed huge. I still struggled with speaking and remembering, and now we had these spelling test all the time. Heck, spelling tests were awful. I worried a lot about my strangeness and found myself alone more and more. I didn't mind being alone. Sometimes life gets too busy. Being alone, I could dream, mostly about dying and coming back a better person—you know, smart.

Outside and away from everyone, I felt free. I forgot about school and how hard it was. We had lots of trees around our house and a forest out back that went right up to the mountain tops. I loved hiking through the trees, and sometimes I would go right over to the rock quarry with a cliff that went a long way down. I was on top of the world up there. I spent as much time after school as I could outside and alone. All my problems went away, and I enjoyed the silence but for the sound of birds or wind blowing through the leaves. Spring, summer, and fall were my favourite times of the year because you could be outside right until the sky turned dark; then I knew it was time to go home.

Winter got so cold, and we lived halfway up one of the mountains of Vancouver, so we got a lot of wet snow. Wintertime at recess, the schools everywhere said that it was now okay for girls to wear pants under their dresses to school—I think I was in grade 7. This was a pretty big thing because it was the start of ladies being able to wear nice pants outside and for work. I didn't like the cold wet snow. I was always felt cold. We didn't have good boots to stay warm. Dad would say, "Money doesn't grow on trees. Turn those lights off." I just knew that we would have to make do.

CHAPTER 3: THE STRANGE DOCTOR

I remembered being examined by a doctor when I was four or five. It was not all that clear, this memory. This doctor man in a white coat was in a small white room, Mom was sitting on a chair, and they were both looking at me. Why was I there? I didn't know if this appointment was for me or Mom. What was it that they wanted from me? I was to take my clothes off. I was about halfway taking off my clothes because Mom helped me, but I moved away when she went for my underwear. I was so scared, wondering what was happening, and Mom was irritated that I was not doing as I was told.

Why was I to take off my clothes? What was it they wanted from me? Backing up away from both the doctor and my mother, I was pressing myself into the corner of the small room, head down, holding tight to my under panties and tank top, saying "No." I didn't want to take my clothes off in front of this strange man wearing white, but Mom was telling me to take my clothes. I was shaking my head and saying no, knowing I'd be in trouble for not doing as I was told and not listening to what Mom was saying.

This man, wearing white, kindly reached out to stop Mom from getting out of her chair and said, "It's okay, there doesn't seem to be anything wrong with her." I was terribly shaken by this event and glad he had stopped Mom from grabbing me and making me stand naked in front of him. Plus, I was really glad that he didn't see anything wrong with me, but I'd no clue as to why I was even here. Mom did calm down and talked with this doctor about me, but I closed my mind off to what they were saying. I didn't remember anything more about this, and to this very day, I've no idea what it was all about.

CHAPTER 4: SUNDAY SPORTS

On Sunday, because Dad worked hard and this was his day, and he watched sports all day until dinner. The games on the TV went from morning until nighttime.

My brother and sister were not allowed into the house, not even to go to the washroom; they had to go on the ground the dirt inside the corral. They were put outside and had to stay outside in this 12-foot corral of dirt. I remembered seeing a picture of it, surrounded by tall evergreen trees, but it was my sister, Nancy, who talked about it. I had no memory of that time. Nancy said Dad built this round fence out of crossed logs, which he said was to keep the wildlife away. It was like a kiddie corral, and they were not allowed to leave this area, for their own safety because there were black bears walking around from time to time.

I never went into this kiddie corral because I was a lot younger and it was gone by the time I grew up. I was kept in my bedroom. Nancy told me this about their corral

I can remember once, when I was old enough to be outside, my sister and I were peeking in the living room window. It was Sunday, and we could hear the sports on the TV. Nancy was really mad about being left outside, and she was not afraid to say so. I followed her around like a lost dog. There were no neighbours living around us, and lots of trees and a dirt road running by the front of our house. Trees across the road, heck, everywhere you looked there were trees and bushes. However, for me, it was super. I just liked being outside, I so enjoyed the space. There was just so much to see and do, in the great outdoors, and I was thrilled to be outside.

Nancy said she didn't remember much about me when I was a baby because I was kept in my bedroom. So I guess this was why I enjoyed the great outdoors so much. Once I was old enough and knew my way around the forest and our neighbourhood. I wandered around everywhere, climb trees and looked for some great hiding spots, I thought in these hiding places that I could live there. I guess I liked to hide because no one could find me and call me names that always hurt my feelings.

There was this little trickling stream I discovered, way out back in the forest behind the house. The water just came out from the rocks from nowhere, and boy was it ever cold. There were ferns and moss growing over and around these rocks, and once close enough you could hear a gentle trickling sound. I would dream that I could live right there by this little creek and no one would ever know I was there. I always felt happy by this little creek deep in the woods. It was a safe and wonderful place to dream. I would pretend there were little people who lived there and I would leave bread crusts, hoping that they would one day come out and play with me. I would talk to them, and they didn't care that I couldn't pronounce words correctly. It was a place where I felt belonged.

CHAPTER 5: ELEMENTARY SCHOOL

I struggled. I was not like the other kids at all. This was pretty clear to everyone in school as well as at home. Grade two, I have only a few memories, mostly staying after school because I just wasn't getting math, and my teacher was trying to help me understand. The teacher wasn't being mean with me; I think she really wanted to help me. I felt so lost, sitting alone at my desk. Other kids were outside playing or had gone home. I just wanted to go home to my little creek and cry. I would look at those numbers in front of me, but it meant nothing to me. I had no idea how to add or subtract; it was almost like they jumped around on the page.

When in sports at school, if I played hard I had dizzy spells and I would fall to the ground. My friends just thought I was clumsy, and I would get up as fast as I could, saying, "I'm okay." It didn't matter to me if my legs were bleeding from my fall because I didn't want them to think I was a cry baby; it seemed important to me that I fit in. There was something wrong with me. Even in sports I was clumsy, but I enjoyed school enough because of the other kids. I knew that they were a lot smarter than I was, and I wondered why.

I had heard my parents talking about how Nancy (my sister, who was almost four years older than me) was having some troubles in school too. I felt less alone, kind of like we had something in common.

It was not just me, and I wondered if Nancy was having a hard time with her memory too. Nancy and I were not close. She seemed to have so many problems and was always fighting with Mom about something. I knew this because Mom had told me that she wasn't a happy child like me. I felt closer to Mom because she seemed to understand me and this made me feel special, like I was her favourite.

I was sitting at my desk this one day in school. I could hear the chalk clicking on the blackboard while the teacher was writing. All of us students were sitting quietly, watching the teacher writing things down. Everything went black. I froze in total darkness! There was no warning. I didn't feel any different. Everything just went black. Not a sound, only darkness. I held onto my desk, pressing my body forward. I didn't want to fall because everyone in class would know that there was something wrong with me. I didn't know if I had closed my eyes or if they were wide open. Blackness where have I gone?

Once I could see again, I internalized. I went deep inside myself, but nothing was there. I was a total blank. It was a terrible feeling. Next thing, I know a girl sitting in the next desk beside me whispered, "Are you alright?" I didn't know how she knew I was in trouble or if I was making some small kind of sound, but she was the first sound I heard.

I couldn't answer her and I didn't know what to say. I was totally and utterly lost, empty, nothingness. I swallowed, but I had no moisture, I think because my mouth was partially open. I didn't know this girl's name, and I knew that I should know her name. *Why can't I remember her? What's happening to me?* I was in an empty place, all alone inside my body. Fear was what followed. I just kept looking and thinking that I should know her name. Over and over again in my head, I asked myself, *why didn't I know her? What's happening to me?* I didn't speak. I just sat there, empty.

The teacher finished up with the chalk, turned around, and started to talk. I looked up at her and thought, *Oh no, who are you? I should* know the teacher's name. *I should know what she is doing and saying. What is happening to me? Blank. Why don't I know these things? Why did the room go black and no one else see this?* I just wanted to crawl into a ball and never be seen again.

The teacher spoke, but I had no idea who she was or what she was talking about. Everything she wrote on the blackboard was gone. Everything in my mind was gone. I had no clue what was going on, but the teacher didn't notice me acting strange. I didn't remember if this happened to me more than this one time. I didn't know how I made it home, and I sure wasn't going to say anything because I was already a problem.

I did fail grade three. I was called a dummy at school and stupid when I got home. I spent more time at the little creek in the forest, the little creek that seemed to come out of nowhere, just like me.

Nancy, my sister, had a nick-name too; her nick-name was meathead. "Nothing but meat in her head." And I got "Hey, stupid, dinner is ready." It was mostly Dad who called us these names and sometimes my brother. I didn't remember Mom calling me stupid nor do I remember Mom saying stop, so I would just drop my head down and try hard not to hear what my sister or I were being called. Nancy would get mad and go pout, sitting in the living room chair. Dad would say this in disgust in a negative way and walk away from us, leaving us to worry and wonder what we had done to make him unhappy with us.

Sad was a feeling my sister and I carried, both then and now.

CHAPTER 6: CRUSHING NIGHTMARES

I was having these awful nightmares. I was not exactly sure when they started, but I do know I had them a lot and they were really scary. I would be lying in my bed, almost asleep, and could hear the sound of crushing rubber, like the glue my brother used when he was making up his models. Evan had some pretty cool models, monsters from the horror movies we watched. One was a swamp monster, and one was a mummy. He would paint them too. Evan had an eye for art and painting. I think it was the sound of that rubber glue he used, tightly squeezed; as I lay there, I would slip into a nightmare where the walls of my room were squeezing down hard on the rubber, getting closer and closer. The problem was I couldn't move. All I could do was lie there until I was crushed.

My memory was always failing me and speaking words, it would be like only half the words came out. Why can't get my tongue around these new words? Even if someone tried to break words down for me, I still had a hard time of it. I worried about these strange nightmares and my bad memory, but at bedtime I would go to bed feeling sleepy, and for no apparent reason, a mysterious and unidentified monster would stalk me in my sleep. My bedroom was warm, and it was still light outside. I would lay my head down on the pillow. It was the sound of crushing rubber, really hard-pressed rubber! I had no awareness of falling asleep, but I must have because before I knew it, there was the morning sun coming through the bedroom window.

I was not sure when that strange rubber sound turned into other nightmares. In fairness, my mom did take me to the doctors to find out what was wrong with me and why I was not growing fast enough. I had boils on my legs a few times; Dad also had boils, and I think maybe I ended up with them because I was the last to use the bathwater. Dad always had his bath first, then we three kids would follow. "Hot water costs money," Dad would say. I had sties in my eyes; I can remember having to wear an eye patch more than once to elementary school, because of this sty in my eye. I had them quite a few times. My hair was always dirty, with a greasy look to it, and itchy.

Oh yes, and the school sports day, I would have sunstroke. I really liked sports day because it was okay to run around, plus there were so many other kids to play with and things to eat like popsicles and hot dogs. But before it was all over, I would be so sick, Dad and Mom would have to take me home a bit early. I think it was my seventh year when Mom gave me a hat and I didn't get sick. Allergies were just something I'd always had, and bad sinuses. I cringed at the thought of cold season because of head colds; I almost felt panicky. Mom gave me lots of Chlor-Tripolon allergy pills, but they made me so sleepy.

CHAPTER 7: OKANAGAN FRUIT

Dad would take Evan (my brother, not quite six years older than me) up to the Okanogan to buy fruit in the summertime. Mom and my self plus Nancy would just stay at home, and I was okay with this as Mom didn't care what we were doing. Nancy wondered why she couldn't go with Dad and her brother Evan; she was old enough. Mom said it was for father and son to do, that's why, end of story. Nancy didn't like this. She asked questions, demanding an answer. It hurt me to watch her do this because Nancy always looked so heartbroken by Mom's answer. I didn't know if Nancy ever asked these question to anyone other than Mom. I asked questions of my friends at school. Some kids didn't like answering all my many questions. I would wonder how my friends remembered their phone numbers. I needed it written down so I could see it. Then I would have to really work hard to get my head around it. Nancy had a much better memory than me.

So when Nancy asked why she couldn't go with Evan and Dad to buy fruit, I knew that this would be upsetting and would hide somewhere until the house was quiet. Dad and Evan would be coming home with fruit, and this was a good thing because Dad would put all these peaches and pears over the ping-pong table in our basement to ripen up. I was a little better than eye level, gazing up and picking just the right ones to hide and eat. You had to move the fruit around some, that way Mom didn't know you were eating up her fruit. I thought this was wonderful, the smell of fresh fruit ripening in our basement.

Mom said that this fruit was for her canning and that it would give us fruit to eat all winter long. So I wasn't to eat any more, but sometimes I just had to eat some. When it did come time for canning, I would stand on a chair for what felt like hours, helping with the peeling at the kitchen sink. But I didn't mind because I like helping Mom out. It made her happy. I was her special helpful little girl. When Mom wasn't looking, I would sneak a taste, so this made it all worthwhile. Hey, all of us kids would sneak fruit out of the basement. It wasn't just me!

We did have a lot of fun with the ping-pong table. Well, Evan and Nancy did. I was no good at it but would watch them play for hours. This was a happy time, watching them play ping-pong, because of the laughter. We didn't hear laughter much at home, or if we did it was because someone was teasing, which meant someone wasn't happy. This was fun, running around the ping-pong table, hitting the little white ball on your turn, huffing and puffing. It was so fun to watch. We played card games, too. I didn't think I ever won a game, but I was just happy when they would let me play.

Dad had built this zip line in our back yard. I was too small play on it, but Evan and Nancy went on it. I think it was Evan who went first and smacked into the house, so Dad would have to catch you before that; thus, it wasn't long before that zip line was gone. Dad had a good imagination for this sort of stuff, even a tree swing that went way out into the air. This was in the front yard off a branch of a big evergreen. I didn't try this out because it went way out over a hill and I was too little to hang on. I watched the other kids having fun; even other kids came to ride around on the swing. Nancy had her turn, but something went wrong, and her pants slide down so her underpants were showing. She was dreadfully upset. All the other kids were laughing at her. She was madly crying to Mom, saying, "Why don't we have any good clothes?"

When Dad said no, I didn't talk back. When Dad spoke you listened, and there would be no questions. All of us kids listened when Dad spoke; maybe it was his tone.

I have a small memory of my parents doing forest wardens with Evan and Nancy. It was Girl Guides, but this all stopped by the time I grew up because of another interest. Dad started singing. I did a lot of watching of the goings-on but was never quite old enough to do anything. I thought it was great that my parents did this forest warden stuff because sometimes we would go on camping trips and stay in these big cabins with all the other kids. I remember I was the youngest of the group and I was put in the cabin with the other kids, in rows of bunk beds. Fresh air and the smell of these cabins were super. There was a lake with canoes. As it turned out, I really liked canoeing. It was beautiful the way the water moved over the paddles, with large yellow lilies peeking out of the lake's edges—such big, round, wet-looking, dark green leaves. I wasn't allowed to go out on the lake by myself, so I talked this other younger girl with the most beautiful name, Roxanne, into going with me. We got in trouble because it was just getting dark when we hit the shore, but it was worth it.

CHAPTER 8:
NO ROUGHHOUSING

Mom told me I was not a planned baby. She was on a new birth control and it didn't work. I had asked Mom because one of my friends was talking about that. Mom said, when I asked her with a friend, "Lots of ladies got pregnant around the same time. The government decided that there was a need for more children in Canada so they put out bad birth control. It was to make us woman have more babies." So this was why Evan and Nancy are so much older than me. Yup, I figured I was an unplanned baby.

I was still not doing well in school, struggling with my memory and new words. It was the mid to late 60s. Mom said to Nancy, "Girls don't need an education. You just need to get a man and have babies." Nancy heard this a lot more than I did, right up until she left the house and rented her own apartment. Dad wasn't allowed to do any roughhousing with us girls because Mom said, "You may ruin the girls from having babies." Mom really wanted Nancy to have babies.

Dad, however, would roughhouse with Evan. Year after year, a lot! I can remember sitting on the sofa, curled into a little ball, worrying about Evan and our dog barking like crazy. Dad would make all kinds of jokes while he pinned Evan to the floor over and over again. You could hear them puffing away and Dad would say things like, "He's got me now. I can't move." But I could see that this was not true and I would smile a stressful smile. Evan really tried hard to win, put everything into it, but it was just too much for him. Dad would have Evan pinned down over and over again, sitting on top of him. Sometimes the dog would bite at Dad, barking wildly to make them stop. I was glad when it was over, I didn't move from my spot on the sofa watching, they didn't care I was in the room. Evan was gone from the room fairly fast when Dad let him go, and so was I. Then I could breathe again, I was glad that we girls didn't have to do all this roughhousing.

CHAPTER 9:
THE BAD HOUSE

Our house was called the "bad house" by the other kids at school, and none of my friends liked to come to my house after coming by only once. I guessed it was because Evan would scare the daylights out of them but even this I didn't quite understand. Evan was always up to something.

I thought our house looked like all the others that were now showing up all along our street. Dad had planted flowers, and our grass was always cut nice. I even mow the lawn with one of those manual rotary lawnmowers. The hills were really hard to do because I was so little, so Dad bought me a brand new lawnmower. It was small enough for me, and it was electric, so I was to watch what I was doing and not run over the cord. I tried to do as much as I could to help out because it would make Dad and Mom happy. I tried very hard to make up for the things I wasn't good at.

We were pretty much on our own at nighttime as Dad and Mom went out, and my brother looked after my sister and myself. However, Evan was always up to something, like pillow fighting. I thought this was awful because I was too little to fight back and would be knocked down over and over, so I would go to bed and fast. Evan enjoyed scaring us. He also liked hiding under the bed and would jump out. We'd yell, "Evan, stop that." Then he was done and would go watch TV.

Dad sold some of the land beside our house and right out back, so now other kids were moving in on our street. Evan liked to scare these kids too. No one messed with my brother and this made me feel safe. Evan was my protector. I never worried about any kids picking on me because they were scared of my brother.

Our parents were gone a lot with Dad's new singing career. They were very busy, five nights a week. I went with them once I got older mainly because I didn't want to be home alone. Most nights we didn't get home until way after midnight. Mom would say if I was too tired I could skip my morning classes. I didn't because I like going to school.

However, with people moving in my quiet little creek was not as unseen as it had been before, so I was careful about not being seen going there. I enjoyed the guiltless pleasure of the small trickling stream. I could act silly, laugh, or cry and try to forget all the things that made no sense to me, but mostly I would practice saying new words. I so struggled with new words.

Sometimes, on a hot day, I would untie my laces and slip out of my runners, sighing loudly from the icy cold water as I dipped in my feet. I wished that I was smarter and I wished that I was prettier like my sister as I looked down at my matchstick legs. I had fuzzy blonde hair that was always so messy. I was both nervous and embarrassed at the fact I was so stupid. *Why am I not like the other kids?* I couldn't make sense of it, and this bothered me so much my voice caught in my throat. I would choke to fight back tears, pressing my hand to my eyes to stop myself. I would try to put this all out of my head. Time passed and I tried to let it go.

I turned my face up so the sun coming through the trees warmed me and I could see the birds flying from branch to branch. I so enjoyed sitting by that little stream. There would also be times that I would worry about those awful nightmares and wonder why. I didn't have a lot of friends, and I didn't remember any of us ever having many friends in our house when we were little. If one of my friends came to the door, I would yell, "I'm going to the park," and would be gone. I knew that I was to be home before dark, and I didn't recall introducing my friends to my mom. Evan did have friends over but not until he was a teenager from high school. Then there was lots of stuff going on around our house and sometimes parties. Every one of my brother's friends was nice to me, and I liked that part. Even looking back now, Evan has some really good friends. I could go to bed knowing everything would be okay because my brother would never let anyone hurt me.

Evan went into high school. It was a lot farther away from our house. Our little school was only a few blocks away, but it only went as high as grade 7. The high school was over a mile away. It went from grade 8 until grade 12. For one year, Nancy would be in grade 7 when I went into grade 1. Evan would tease her to no end about being in the same school as me. I was happy that Nancy and I would be in the same school, but I quickly learned she did not feel the same way. Nancy didn't want to be seen with her little sister.

We did not get along she was always mad about something, and I was always happy—well, tried to be. This one time I couldn't find a shirt to wear, so I foolishly picked out one of my sister's. Now, I didn't pick just any shirt I borrowed her good one or should I say her favourite one. Nancy saw me in her shirt. She was not happy and wanted me to take it off right then, but I talked her into waiting until I got home first. I never borrowed another one of her shirts again.

{Wow, sorry, I just saw our age difference. Nancy was six years older than me. See, this shows how things are for me. It took me years to see that Evan and Dad play fighting was an awful thing because it was so normal for me. I had never put 2 + 2 before. To this day, birthdays are still very much a sore spot. Wow.}

I was not invited to other kids' parties, and I stayed close to home because at least my dad and mom understood that there was something wrong with me. Not that they ever talked to me about it, but

I could tell by the way I was treated and the looks I got. My whole family knew that I was not very smart so I tried to be funny in hopes of making up for it. Evan liked being scary. He even did up our house this one Halloween night. It was so spooky kids ran from our house, dropping their bags and running. Mom went after them and gave back their bags, which lasted a long time because they went out for the night. However, the next year we ended up with hundreds of kids or more, so Evan put speakers in the bushes and would speak loudly and make them jump, plus had things fly out from the trees at them. Children would hang onto their Halloween bags and run. So, yes, Evan was always up to something but I thought he was the greatest.

CHAPTER 10: MORE NIGHTMARES

Nightmares took me to the edge of madness on so many a long lonely night. I believed these nightmares were in my life just to mock me. I would wake soaked in sweat, heart pounding. Were they simply my wild imagination? I guess I must have said something about my nightmares because it seemed to me Mom told her friends more than once that I have a vivid imagination. I didn't talk to anyone about them. It was one of those things you just learned to live with, but some nights I would summon the courage to get out of bed and look out my window at the stars. It was so peaceful. I liked looking up at the sky at night. This helped take away my fears. Sometimes I would even open up my window to let in the fresh air.

The days passed and the seasons changed, and I still could not remember things I had just heard and still had a hard time saying new words. I would go out and sit in the woods by my little creek and practice words over and over again. Practicing sometimes helped, and sometimes it didn't. I could not spell to save my life, but I really didn't want my life saved anyway. We would have these spelling tests; it was pretty sad the way I spelled. I would get so nervous that I didn't think I could even spell my own name.

I really didn't know why I was there, and I didn't know why I was so different. I would dream that I could die and come back as a better person and these awful nightmares would be gone forever. In the mornings, when I woke from these nightmares, I would rub my fingers through my hair, deeply lost in thought and feeling very much drained and absolutely isolated. I would tell myself, *I'm going to be alright.*

What's wrong with me? I had no one to speak to about these things because I watched how awful life was for my sister when she tried to understand what was going. So I thought it best to do as I was told and I learned that this was how things were. Nancy and I were not close. She seemed to be having her own kind of problems, and she spoke out often.

CHAPTER 11: THE POEM

I had learned a poem in school, and my teacher said, "If you say this poem when your parents are fighting, they will stop." It was a cute little rhyming poem that was supposed to make you smile. I remembered this little poem and worked it over lots in my mind. I believed that saying this poem would somehow work and Dad and Mom would stop arguing.

This one day I came home from elementary school. Dad and Mom were in the living room fighting. I went right beside them and sang out this poem loud and clear just like I was told to by my teacher. Dad backhanded me in the face, and I flew and hit my back on our sofa. Shocked, I crawled under the kitchen table, and they fought on. I cried and made my way to bed when no one was looking. No one noticed me, and I felt no one cared and cried myself to sleep. What I did learn was school was not going to teach me what I needed to know. An extremely hard lesson.

I said to Mom later in the week that I didn't like school anymore, but it was okay because Mom told me that girls didn't need an education. We just had to get a man and have babies. This made me feel better because school was really hard. I had to sit in corners or out in hallways because I would ask other kids too many questions.

EMILY KNEW

The other poem I was to find in a particular book. Everyone in class got one. We had to choose one, then we would have to remember it and stand in front of class, reciting it. I was really worried about standing in front of the class and not remembering, so I searched this book over for the smallest poem there was. It's funny, but I still remember it:

My mother killed me,
My father picked up the bones,
My little sister buried me under the ivory stones.

Author Unknown

This was the poem I read in front of my class.

CHAPTER 12: IRONING

Mom was ironing her clothes to go out for the night. She always looked so pretty in her new dresses. Dad had started practising singing songs in the basement, and I would listen, but not to close, while Dad sang. He always looked happy when he was doing this, and I really enjoyed watching. I thought that Dad was the best singer ever.

This one night, Dad was having his shower and Mom was ironing her dress with the TV on. I was standing close to Mom, watching her work on the bright-coloured dress that matched Dad's shirt. Mom ironed Dad's shirt earlier before her dress because she had to look after Dad.

I was little, standing at chin level next to the ironing broad, and had taken the hanger Mom had out and was balancing it on my tongue. The curled end of this hanger was on the tip of my tongue, and I was standing up on my tiptoes. I didn't know why I was doing this, but when Mom saw this, she grabbed the hangar, giving me no time to respond, and turned it. "Don't put that in your mouth." Then she ripped it away from me.

My eyes flew open. I immediately knew something was wrong. I was moving back at the same time as she did this. Mom never gave me a second look, even as blood spilled into my mouth. She had torn the inside of my cheek open. "Ouch," I said, and my hand went up to my lips. She had momentarily stopped ironing, and her only response was, "And that's why you don't put things into your mouth." She didn't look at me, but she knew she had hurt me.

Mom went back to her ironing and watching TV, and I backed away, not knowing what to do. So I just sat on our sofa, running my tongue over the big cut inside my mouth and tasting my own blood. A vague feeling of distrust sunk in. Sitting still and quiet, I was quite lost in thought and trying hard to ignore the hurt feelings rolling around in my head. Dad and Mom went out for the night, and I sat there feeling sorry for myself for some time. I knew that there was something not right about what had just happened, but what?

CHAPTER 13: DAD & MOM

I spent much of my youth following Dad around when he was home working on the car or in the yard planting flowers. Dad was the one who showed me how to take the dead flowers off so new ones would grow back, pansies with little faces on them. I liked the look of those flowers with the little faces. I really liked following Dad around because he would talk to me sometimes. Mom, however, didn't like gardening or flowers or any yard work. I never saw her outside looking at them. Mom did like the trees Dad planted. They grew and blocked the view of the dirt road. It wasn't a busy road, but I guess Mom liked her privacy. Once they sold the two extra lots they owned, Dad built a big fence around our back yard. I was told it was called the "people haters fence" because you couldn't see inside or outside.

Together Dad and Mom would pick up trees from the places we went camping at. We kids slept in the car and Dad and Mom the tent. Nancy didn't like to go camping because she said she always got stuck doing the dishes in cold water; she said her hands hurt. Nancy would show her shrivelled fingers. Evan didn't have to do dishes because he was a boy.

Dad built our house and did a lot of yard work to make our house look nice, and I have a memory of a big boat that Dad was going to build, but he sold it before he ever got it done, said that one day he would just sail away. It sat like a skeleton of a whale for a long time beside our house. One day, it just disappeared. Dad had sold it and turned that space into a carport. This carport roof was flat and made it perfect for Nancy to sneak out the window at night if she wanted to, and I think she did. I used to climb out on this roof just to look around. I loved standing tall over everything, maybe because I was so short. Mom never said anything about us climbing on the roof. As long as we weren't bothering her we could do what we wanted. She didn't seem to care what we were up to because she was always having coffee with the new neighbour lady or lying with her feet up watching TV. Mom said her legs hurt, so she had to have her feet up on the sofa. Dad was gone off to work, and some nights he didn't come home, leaving us alone with Mom. I didn't remember much about our times together with Mom I think I was pretty much sent to my room and to bed. Mom liked to watch a lot of movies.

    Dad would tell great stories about his job when we had company. His stories always got a good laugh from his friends. Dad also showed his company how to solve puzzle games; these were tricky kinds of games. He was a great entertainer for the right crowd, meaning the people who adored him when he was singing. When Dad and Mom brought company home late at night after his singing was over, he was way less stressful to be around, and these people seemed to really like him and how smart he was with these fun puzzle games. I would sit on the floor and listen in, and sometimes I would be included. It made me feel smart that I could figure them out before the other adults.

    Mom was a beautiful woman and always seemed lost or would drop things sort of goofy. She was almost playful. I thought that some of these people felt sorry for her in some way. Mom played dumb around these people, innocent and caring. She one time had hidden Dad's money in the flip-up toaster and burned it in the morning. She then went to the bank in a hurry telling them what she had done. They gave her some other money because they could make out the numbers on her bills. Later, this would the joke told to their friends. Mom seemed a little goofy. Like Lucille Ball, I heard Mom say about herself.

Nancy wondered why Dad could be so nice to all the other people and their kids, yet not so much with us. Nancy would say this to me, but I had no answer at all. Mom said Dad worked hard and that we would be best to leave him alone. Dad was harshly critical and very much so to Nancy, so it was easy enough to do as we were told. He was a strong and scary man. I didn't ever talk back to Dad, and when he spoke I listened. I think Dad didn't like Nancy so much because she asked so many questions. Dad was strict, and Mom made it sound like she feared him. She would say, "Oh, he's going to be mad at me. There is no money in the bank," or "What are we going to do? Dad thinks there's money and there isn't." It was always about money. I felt we were to somehow look out for Mom; she always had money troubles. Mom always seemed to be helping Evan out, and they were very close to each other like he was to protect her from Dad.

Dad did have a good laugh and a real smile. Mom didn't laugh like Dad and Mom didn't laugh much at all that I remember. Mom was not a smiley person nor was she sad. She always seemed busy getting someone coffee or cookies when guests were around. I guess because she worried about money so much Mom wasn't smart either, but kind of a goofy lady. When she was at home alone, and Dad was working she would say how tired she was lying on the sofa with her feet up because she said her legs were sore, so we would just leave her alone. Another thing she was always doing was pushing her nose up. She said she wanted a cute turned-up nose. I thought she looked silly doing this. She didn't ever play or listen to music. Never once did I see my mom run to the radio because it was a song she liked, nor do I remember her singing or enjoying music ever, but she did like her movies.

I do remember fighting with Nancy for the plastic bread bags when it was raining. Who am I kidding? She would always win when it was raining, and it rained a lot. We would wear plastic bags because of the holes in the bottom of our boots. I would have to get and hide these plastic bags before Nancy knew there were any. I sure didn't like sitting with wet cold feet in school all day, but I understood that we didn't have any money, so it was what it is.

Nancy would ask Mom questions. It didn't ever look like Mom cared about things. She struggled so hard to understand. I would watch and wonder why Nancy bothered do this because she would never get any answers that made sense. Mom needed pretty new clothes when she was off with Dad. Singing was as good as it was going to get. "How come we don't have any pretty clothes like you do?" Nancy asked. Or this one, which Nancy asked and went on for years: "Why can't you remember my birthday?" or "Why can't you remember what day I was born?" Mom most times just didn't answer, and I never could understand why this bothered Nancy so much. Who cares what day you're born on? Nancy asked this last one a lot, why don't you remember what day I was born?" I was standing just around the corner, out of the way but peeking in just the same. I figured Mom had a bad memory like me. *Why was Nancy asking this?* Nancy was crying her heart out, and I could feel her heart breaking, but Mom was undisturbed by Nancy's cries, almost smiling the way she did. I searched mom's face for any signs of understanding, clutching my arms together over my chest and leaving nail marks on my skin. I couldn't take my eyes away from mom's oh-so-calm face. My only defence was to finely look away, feeling weighed down and very sad. I didn't think I was in elementary school yet; I was pretty young.

It was terrible for my sister and constantly on her mind. My eyes hooded over as I could feel her emotions, her heartbreak. That vague distrust I quickly tried to ignore. It makes me sad, but every October Nancy would ask again: "Mommy why don't you remember what day

I was born?" I would worry for Nancy. I knew this would not end well for her and it sure never did. Mom would just dismiss her with a glance or answer in a very monotone voice "I don't know." Mom used "I don't know" all the time, so Nancy eventually stopped asking.

CHAPTER 14: SKELETONS IN THE CLOSET

Dad and Evan fought a lot, it seemed to me, over tools, and some of these were terrible fights with blood on the basement floor and Evan taking off in his car to join Mom's family upcountry. He really liked it up with our maternal grandfather. He did go and spend some time up there this one summer when he was seventeen and could drive a car. Evan was all ready to make the move upcountry. Grandpa would help him get a job. He was a man's man, hunting and fishing. He would talk with Evan and tell him stories about the war. They would even sit down and share a drink together and some laughs. I think it was the first time Evan felt like a man. He had come home excited about moving, but Mom said some not nice things about her family.

Mom told me and my brother about this separately, on different occasions. Evan shouldn't go upcountry to live because when Mom was a little girl, her dad would get drunk and come into her room and would shake the bed to wake her up, and this one time her dad had even stuck his fingers into her. Mom told me about this the next day or so because I had asked if Evan was moving.

I was quite shocked at the way she told me about what had happened. I knew this was not a good thing, but I was too young to understand what she was talking about and didn't know why she was telling me about this. This was bad, so I guessed Evan wasn't moving away.

Many years later, when my brother and sister were married, we were looking at a picture of Grandpa, Evan told me what Mom had told him. I said that I knew and that Mom had told me about Grandpa. However, Evan only said that Grandpa had molested her: there was nothing in his account of what had happened about Grandpa sticking his fingers inside Mom.

We felt sorry for Mom. What had happened was a very sad thing, and we tried to understand her upbringing. Now we had a reason for why Mom was the way she was. No more needed to be said. Many years later, just before I stopped all contact with my mother—and this was the main reason I stopped all contact—we were visiting with other family members and my uncle, Mom's brother, and he was showing Mom pictures of their dad when he was younger. We had a very nice lunch together and a good time.

As I was driving Mom home from visiting, I asked her, "Was hard for you to look at pictures of your dad?" I was thinking maybe she would now be able to let go of some of the hurt she had gone through as a child.

"No. Why? What are you talking about?" Mom truly had no idea what I was saying.

"I was wondering if you found it hard to look at him. After all, he had molested you when you were a young girl."

"What are you talking about? He didn't molest me!" She spoke without thinking.

"You said that he came drunk into your room and would shake your bed and that he had molested you!"

Mom stared straight ahead, looking lost. She sat motionless, then said, too calmly, "Oh no. You've got it wrong."

"Evan thinks that Grandpa molested you because that's what you told him." I shot back. I was having a really hard time understanding what was happening.

"Well," she said, "he's got it wrong, too! It was a neighbour who had done that."

I froze up inside. She was so casual about it. My mind was reeling.

Evan really liked Grandpa, but after what Mom said, their friendship had ended. My brother was heartbroken. Even now, I can't find the words to describe how shocked I was to think Mom was that evil. This was her dad she accused of molesting her. I knew right away she had lied. I couldn't get her out of my car fast enough.

Grandpa was gone and there was no getting back with him.

Mom could not remember all her lies! It's just so awful. Writing this down now, I have tears in my eyes. Evan could have had a much better life, but she didn't want him to move away from her. Evan had always been Mom's little protector, and to this day she keeps him as close as she can. *Who does this sort of thing?* I felt sick. I was holding back things because it just hurt so much.

I did not tell my brother because of two things. First, Mom liked to tell me things because she knew that no one would believe me. After all, there was something wrong with me. Second, the other thing that I worried about was if my brother might do something like kill her for being the awful person that she is. He still thinks that she has been badly hurt, so even though she drives him nuts, he cares for her. I couldn't live with myself if he cracked, but who could blame him.

Later, once I was home—and I was really glad we were so close to home when I had asked her about Grandpa—I sat in disbelief. You know why? I think my mother said that her father had "stuck his fingers in her" so that I would never tell this story to anyone. By the way, this is the very first time I've let this out … Oh, God!

CHAPTER 15: SECRETS & HIDING PLACES

Nancy was told by Mom to always hide the mail before Dad could see it. Mom told her that men didn't need to know everything. When she was young and at home, Nancy was the secret keeper for Mom; she was told she was the only one that Mom could trust. Nancy always helped Mom this way; she felt close to Mom because of this, I guessed.

Nancy one day had shown me the best hiding spot ever. It was our secret. We went downstairs, and into the laundry room. Nancy said, "This is a great spot," and she removed some broads from the laundry room wall, and I followed her under the house. It was called the crawl space. I was thrilled that she would share this with me. The broads could go back, and no one would ever know you were under the house. Nancy said, before leaving me, "Make sure you put the broads back when you leave."

I stayed under the house to just get the feeling of being there. It was a very safe place to be. Everything seemed pretty good in the house as I knew how to make people laugh, and now I had the best hiding place ever. I liked to design or create funny little critters and things out of nothing; could work on these for hours. I did sit and play under the house on more than one occasion, sometimes to play but sometimes to hide.

I would hear Mom say to her friends that I was such a happy child. Mom liked when I would sit quietly and make things. This would always put a smile on my face. Times like this, my troubles would just melt away. Even my nightmares would be forgotten. In my world, only the sun was shining and the birds were singing. Life couldn't get any better. I knew how to not ask too many questions and how to hide, and Mom liked it when I was happy. So happy I was.

CHAPTER 16: LOCKED DOORS

My job at home was to make sure doors were locked each night. This wasn't a job that my parents or anyone put on to me. I did it out of necessity, for my own safety. It's kind of funny as I didn't know why I needed safety, but it became apparent as I wrote this and remembered. I watched a lot of horror shows with my brother and sister and alone late in the dark of night.

It seemed to me that half the battle would be to lock every door and to know good hiding spots. The problem was I didn't have a good memory, so I keep wondering, did I lock the basement door or not? The front and back doors were easy ones, straight across from the other with a long hallway between, but the basement door was quite another thing. There were no lights on in the basement, so if I forgot or needed to check if I locked this door, that meant I had to make it down the stairs to turn on the light. Many a time I would have to check, and sometimes I would double-check just to make sure. I wouldn't leave the light on because that way if someone did break in, I knew my way around our house in the dark of night.

I would be lying in my bed asleep and hear pounding on the basement or front door by Nancy or Evan to unlock the door and let them in. It was creepy waking up to the sound of someone screaming your name.

CHAPTER 17: CLOTHES MAKE THE WOMAN

Dad and Mom are heading out the door soon as Mom was finished ironing her beautiful dress. Nancy in her big chair by the living room window, not looking happy and asking Mom why she had to babysit me. I always felt small and sad that she felt this way, but there really was nothing that I could do. Evan had gotten another job other than babysitting across the street, which he did for a few years. Mom said Evan needed to make his own money. Once Dad and Mom left it wasn't long before Evan, and sometimes Nancy, were out the door.

Mom had beautiful dresses, and Dad had matching shirts; they looked wonderful. Five nights a week as Dad had become quite a good singer and they were teaching some dance moves, but mostly Mom would be making the coffee and putting out cookies. My parents even came into schools to teach some of those dance moves. Mom was a beautiful woman, her hair done just so. I didn't ever remember seeing her without make-up on and her hair done. I think this was when Mom was her happiest. So it seemed odd that Mom never listened to music other than with Dad.

Nancy, however, didn't see it that way. She was frustrated that she didn't have pretty clothes too. Nancy would ask, "How come we don't have any nice clothes like you do? Why is it that we only get hand-me-down clothes?" This bothered Nancy to no end but me not so much. I just didn't like the fighting and could put up with anything. Besides we always got a new outfit for the start-up of school.

    Mom thought that Nancy was a bit of a troublemaker and didn't understand why she was such an unhappy girl. Then her face filled with pimples when she became a teenager and this made her even more-unhappy. Whenever Mom could get her hands on her, they would be working on Nancy's face, washing and steaming. Mom took her to the doctors to try to find out what was up with her pimples and get some face wash. I would just get the heck out of the way. My face had some pimples, but I was nothing like Nancy. The stuff that the doctor gave her did help, thank goodness. Nancy always seemed upset, so I figured that Mom had it right that she was a lot of trouble. But I too would sneak some of Nancy's face wash, and it worked for me too! Nancy would sit, so moody, in the big living room chair, day after day. Clearly, asking a lot of questions was not a good thing to do.

CHAPTER 18: HOT DOG DAY

We had hot dog day in school, and it smelled so good the day that they are cooking them. I never did have one of those hot dogs because I knew that we didn't have the extra money. I can remember sitting at my desk as if it were not such a big deal, but I sure would have liked to have had one. Mom was always worried about money, so I never said anything about it.

This one hot dog day at school, and I didn't know Mom found out about this because I never bothered to bring home any of those school notices, I was sitting at my desk at lunchtime. In walked my mom, out of the blue. Tinfoil wrap in her hand, she had brought me some homemade French-fries with salt and ketchup on them. They smelled and tasted good too! I had a surprised look on my face, I was sure. She didn't stay, just dropped them off and was gone. Why had Mom done this? I didn't worry about the whys because it was a really nice thing. I was happily kicking my feet back and forth under my desk, smiling yet puzzled too. Mom was like that. When you least expected it, she would do these nice things. Later in life, Nancy said Mom had done that for her as well, she could nice, but it was a strange thing.

* * *

I would come home from school, the house mostly empty. Mom would be having coffee with her friend's house across the road. By the time my brother and sister got home, Mom would be coming home to cook dinner as Dad would be expecting it.

Nancy came home from school, put on her pajamas, and sat down in front of the big living room window with a sour look on her face. Nancy was not a happy child. She said nothing at all through the school week. I think Nancy hated all of us, and for a long time, she stopped asking Mom all those silly questions. I could never understand why she worried about her birthday so much. Heck, I couldn't remember mine either.

Nancy had to set the table. She did this with much complaining, and we would sit down and try to eat what was in front of us. Mom was not a very good cook. I never looked forward to sitting down at our dinner table, but the good news dinner meant Dad and Mom would be leaving the house soon, and it would go back to being just us.

Once they went out the door, we were home alone. All kinds of things went on in our house. I can remember some rare nights of the three of us practising playing cards until the midnight hours, shuffling the deck. I loved those times when we were getting along. Pillow fights—I never did like those because I was little and could hardly hold up the pillow. I didn't remember a lot of toys in our house; we did have some toys, but after about a week, they would just be gone. You just didn't see them again. There were a few times I wished that I could have some toys like the other kids did, but we always had a deck or two of cards. Dad liked having cards in the house, so we always had cards.

CHAPTER 19: CLEANING AND THE LAUNDRY CHUTE

Evan had an idea how to make Dad and Mom happy. He had the perfect idea on how to do this. We three would clean up the kitchen, wax the floors, and everything. We cleaned for hours; it got really dark outside. Evan planned this because they would be bringing company home that night. We were going to give them a happy surprise. Mom didn't like to do the dishes. She would hide dirty dishes in the oven or under the sink. We would pull out the dirty dishes from their hiding spots and clean them. It took some time as the stuff was really stuck on. The floors brightly shone and it smelled clean too. We were pretty proud of ourselves and were tired, when all was said and done. I was asleep by the time our parents got home, but went to bed knowing they would have a very big surprise. Nothing was said about our big clean up, or if it was I didn't hear it.

It wasn't long after that Dad said that they would be bringing home company and how nice it was that we had cleaned up the place. I was really happy about hearing this and a great feeling to hear when we cleaned up made them happy. So we did it again, but this time it didn't feel the same. We didn't seem as excited, maybe because it wasn't going to be a surprise. They lied and didn't bring home company and came home really late. Evan realized they had tricked us. It was just so that we would knock ourselves out cleaning up. Pretty sneaky. Then we got household chores to do after that.

I can remember doing dishes at the sink. I stood on a chair a long time washing dishes. Nancy always got mad that Evan didn't have to help with the dishes because it was women's work. Evan had other things to do with Dad, and sometimes he went to work at Dad's nighttime job. But at the kitchen sink, Evan would tease us and snap us with a rolled-up towel. Nancy got mad about this kind of stuff a lot. It hurt when you got snapped with that towel. I didn't mind doing the dishes if it would make everybody happy. So I stood on that chair and did dishes until the water turned yucky and my cold fingers shrivelled up.

I was cooking pretty young, too, because I can remember sliding a chair, climbing up, and sitting on the counter beside the stove because it made it easier for me to stir what I was cooking. I found a way to make pudding from cornstarch and milk, and then adding unsweetened chocolate plus sugar. I really liked this and made it a lot when no one was home.

Mom cooked the same things on the same nights every dinner for years. She didn't like to cook but had to because of Dad. Mom cooked pot roast with potatoes, carrots, and sometimes canned peas. On Tuesday, she made this stroganoff with corn, this was an okay dish. Then there would chicken or ham with carrots and sometimes Mom's pickled beets. The veggies were always way overcooked, as was the meat. Oh dear, yes, and steak and kidney pie. Yuck!

This one time at our dinner table, Nancy asked for the salt and reached out with her little hand. To my shock and horror, Dad stabbed her in the back of the hand with his fork because she didn't say please. I remember looking down and feeling really worried and sick about that. We were not allowed to talk at our dinner table.

The food was awful, and I remember sitting there, wishing that we didn't need food to live. Evan would sometimes make faces at the table and try to make us girls giggle because it was us girls who would get into trouble. We had to stay at our dinner table until we ate all our food because kids in other countries didn't have any food! Our food tasted so bad. They could have it. As luck would have it, Mom put napkins on the table. I would use them to put my food in when everyone had left the table. Then I would ask to go to the washroom and would flush down the yucky dinner. Evan and Nancy did this with the dog under the table, but Dad and Mom were already on to that.

I liked peanut butter on toast with a glass of milk. I lived on this whenever I could because Mom burned everything she cooked. Burned carrots and they smelled and tasted bad even a little burned. Canned peas she boiled until those little shells came off. It was night after night of the same things. It was awful, and I was really skinny. I could hear Mom scraping the burnt off our toast in the morning, and we stayed in our bedrooms, not bothering to get up to have our breakfast together because we didn't get along as kids. It was better that we didn't see each other in the morning, Mom would say, and she would go back to bed. Dad would already be at work, so we didn't see him at all in the mornings. Once we had all moved away and started our own lives, we started to visit more with each other, but it was still a little strained.

Nancy tells me that Dad used to make pancakes on Sunday mornings. But Mom had said something about Dad waking up her to early when all she wanted was more sleep, so Dad grumbled, and that stopped. Dad would also hang out the laundry with clothespins in the back yard, on the line. Mom said something about this too. What was said, I just have no idea. So it would seem like we never had clean clothes again. Mom didn't like doing the laundry. It was piled high in the laundry room, as high as I stood. I can remember Nancy asking if she could do her own laundry, but Mom said no, and, you guessed it, another fight of why. Mom didn't want her breaking the washer, I think. This was when I would go into one of my many hiding places.

Dad was building our house while Mom was pregnant with me, I was told. He had put in this laundry shoot from the upstairs bathroom to the downstairs laundry room, which was super because I used to practice going down the laundry chute and out the basement door. No one ever knew I had come or gone from the house. I got pretty good at this and fast. I could move around our house, not making a sound. I could climb up hallway walls and sit on the top of doorways. I was so tiny, not a pound of fat on me. This made it even easier for me to disappear into or behind anything. My brother could put me in the roll-away sofa and close it, and I would play frozen until he came back from the store. I knew how to hide inside my own head and would be as safe as safe could be. When Evan came back I didn't make a sound, and I could hear him calling me. He frantically pulled the cushions off the sofa and opened it up fast. I think he thought that he had killed me. He didn't roll me away in the roll-out sofa again. Didn't get me wrong, I loved my brother; there plenty funny times.

Evan was babysitting across the street this one New Year's Eve. I was home alone, waiting for midnight. Every now, and then the kids in the house next to us came outside with fireworks. It was snowy and cold, so we didn't stay outside very long. Evan was across the street. It was the strike of twelve. Other kids came outside, yelling, "Happy New Year," and so did I. We were pretty excited, yelling, "Happy New Year!" from the porches into the street.

A light flicked on where Evan babysat. The neighbourhood went silent, and we all watched. He walked boldly out the front door, heading straight to the edge of the road. He placed his hands up around his mouth and yelled, "Ba humbug!"

He then turned and walked back inside the house, closing the door. Laughter was heard by us kids in the neighbourhood. Evan always did funny things like that. I was very proud of my big brother.

Nancy, who now had to babysit me all the time, didn't talk much when we were together, and I knew she didn't like having me around, so I tried to be quiet around her. She had so many trouble with her shyness, and she didn't like some of the other kids in school. They made fun of her pimples, so we watched TV, and I would sit on the rug Nancy in the big chair by the window.

CHAPTER 20:
THE FIGHTER

Nancy was the fighter; I will give her that. She didn't back down when she thought Mom should be doing more to help her. She put her heart and soul into the many questions, but Mom always looked calm, doing what she was doing, just like Nancy wasn't there.

"Why don't you remember when I was born?" changed to "Why do I have babysit Emily?" It was always something with Nancy. I felt great distress watching her do this. My insides would twist up. Mom would say, "She's your little sister. You should want to look out for her."

It seemed one day Nancy had given up. She stopped fighting. She was troubled, Nancy just fell apart and her face looked shiny from all the washing. I could see she was not doing well. She would walk away in anger. One day, Nancy was trying to get Mom to understand that she was doing really well at sports and that Dad and Mom should come and watch her. Nancy was good at running. "Why don't you and Dad ever come watch me running? Why can't you at least come and give me a ride home like the other kids' parents do?"

I tried even harder to be funny. Funny didn't work on my sister. So we had a deal. I didn't say anything, and I got to live. Nancy had met a girlfriend who moved just up the street and was frequently gone to her house, even staying the nights there as much as she could. I was now on my own.

I was still having these awful nightmares of walls crushing down on rubber. I'd been getting them for years. In fact, I didn't know life without them. I experienced an unbelievable fear, conscious only of a supreme terror. I was sitting up, shuddering, perspiration sticky and wet on my forehead and in my hair. This was a fear I knew well, followed by collapsing back onto my pillow, telling myself it was only a nightmare, and then staring up at the ceiling. Sometimes I couldn't summon the courage to get out of bed. I would just turn restlessly around and around.

It was strange when I heard Mom say, "She's such a happy child." I wondered a lot about those nightmares, and I wondered if I was such a happy child. I thought I was; there was no one around to give me a hard time. When I thought my nightmares were gone, a few months would pass, and then I would get them again.

* * *

Nancy was now stuck babysitting me all the time, and sometimes she even stayed home, but mostly she would be gone to her friend's house. Dad and Mom went out a lot. It was okay by me because we never had pillow fights. Heck, she never knew I was in the room. It was nice when she did stay home in the dark of night. I felt better knowing I was not alone.

However, this one night, my sister stayed home. We were watching TV. I was almost asleep on the rug when Nancy jumped up screaming. She started running into the kitchen, then back into the living room and around the room screaming.

I jumped up and started to run after her, and suddenly she stopped screaming. I had no idea what was going on, but I was running around, following her, saying, "What?" My eyes opened wide and my heart pounded hard in my chest. "What's going on?"

Nancy dove behind the sofa, not saying anything. She was resting on her arms and knees, breathing hard, with a look of fear in her eyes. I ran behind the sofa and did the same thing, looking right into her eyes, mirroring her. *What's going on?*

We didn't move. I only heard my pounding heart. Nancy looked me right in the eyes, then looked mad, sighed, rolled her eyes, and left the sofa and to look out the living room window again. I followed her but at a distance hadn't a clue as to what had just happened, and she was not talking to me.

Nancy said something the following morning to Dad and Mom and was mad about it. "Someone was looking in the window last night. They had on a mask!"

First time I heard what happened. I could tell that this was not going well. Dad and Mom didn't think much about this and were clearly not worried at all. "It was more than likely Evan playing tricks on you."

This upset Nancy, but I never saw anything, so I just didn't know what to think. *Is Nancy making mountains out of molehills?* But she didn't stop there. She asked Evan, and he said it wasn't him. Once again, Nancy shut down and pouted. She said not another word. No one was listening to her but me, anyway. I saw how scared she was when she looked into my eyes.

CHAPTER 21: GROWING STRONG

Evan had started weightlifting to make himself strong. His veins would bulge from his neck and arms. He got into a few fights. Dad and Evan didn't seem to fight anymore. I was glad about that. Evan had a job and started going his own way, plus he started drinking alcohol and had a few parties at the house. Evan had shown kindness to me sometimes, like giving me a ride in his car on a nice sunny day, a little road trip. Evan's misdeeds and temper were never checked by Mom or Dad. He didn't hurt me, so I guess I overlooked them as well. Evan could do whatever he liked it seemed to me, like having parties and bringing other people home to stay with us who needed a place to stay. He was a boy, and we were only girls. As girls, we were to learn our place! "Little girls are to be seen, not heard."

This one night, Evan came running through the front door with two of his friends. He called out for me, and I came running, wondering what was going on.

He said, "A policeman will be knocking at the front door. You are going to open it and say I'm not here and don't let them in!" Then he went to hide with his friends.

This was my big brother, and we looked out for each, so I did as I was told, but I did wonder if the police would get mad at me. The policeman came knocking at the door and asked me if Evan was home. I didn't feel good about this, but I stuck to my story. "No, he's not here." The policeman asked if I was sure. I said I was and soon after the police were gone his friends came laughing and I went to bed, worrying about getting into trouble.

CHAPTER 21
ALONE

This one night everyone was gone from the house. I wondered where everyone is. I was very little in my nightgown, and it was dark outside. The TV volume was down low, and only one lamp was on in the corner. I have no idea where everyone was. I was sitting right close to the armrest of the sofa and wondering where they were. Time went on, and no one came home. *Should I go to bed or just stay awake?* I wanted to fall asleep, and my eyes are fighting me.

I heard a sound, coming from the back part of our house. I thought it was the back door. I sat up at full attention, my eyes wide open. I was trying to be as small as I could be with my heart pounding. Something was going on. I could hear something, but I didn't know what it was. My mind was racing. I knew it wasn't Evan or Nancy because they would be yelling for me to open the door by now. Plus, they didn't often go to the back door. They used the basement or front door. So who was at the back door right now?

Another sound. I was frozen, holding my breath and listening. A deep fear ran up my body. My eyes fought tears. What was this sound? It was a scraping sort of sound or a crunching. What was happening? Puzzled, tears pooling in my eyes, my arms wrapped around my knees, I was rocking back and forth. I was so afraid. Tears were dropping from my eyes down on my knees. *What should I do? What should I do?* My nose filled up, and I was sniffing and sobbing wiping my face on my pyjamas.

The noise didn't stop. I had to do something, but what? I spied the only thing that was close enough, a tiny green ashtray. It just fit in my little hand. I quickly sat back down on the sofa. I felt safer having something in my hand, even though it wouldn't help. The noise coming from the back door was really scaring me.

What was that?

I made myself get off the sofa and scurried over to the long, open living room wall. Being up against the wall made me feel better, but I couldn't stop myself from crying, and I was wondering why I was alone. *Please, someone come home and save me.*

Looking down the length of the wall, I knew I could crawl to the corner and see what was happening. *Oh, but I sure don't want to do this. Please, someone come home.* The noise was getting louder, and my body was shaking. I was pressed up against the wall and it felt cold. I was stopping every few feet, putting my head down to cry with this tiny ashtray pressed tightly in my hand. It was leaving marks. *Where is everybody? Why am I alone? What am I going to do?*

I crawled along the wall, but my nightgown kept getting stuck on my knees. I stopped and pulled it away. My face was so wet with tears it was getting hard to see. I could hear that strange sound again. *What was that?* I knew I had to know. I didn't want to do this. *I just want someone to please come home. Please!* Finally reaching the end of the longest wall, I had to work up the nerve to look around the corner.

The sound was getting louder and louder. I just needed to give one little peek. I think I might throw up. I was gasping and sobbing and trying not to make too much noise. I didn't peek around the corner because I couldn't take my eyes off the knife blade I had just seen cutting the wood away from the door frame of our back door. My eyes were frozen, watching the back door. All I saw was the flash of a big knife blade slipping back into the darkness. It just disappeared, and there was not another sound.

I didn't know how long I looked at the back door, wondering and listening, but I couldn't move. Was the basement door locked? Was the front door locked? Were all the windows closed? Every nerve in my body seemed broken. It was scary to see a knife cutting away at the back door. But now, where were they? It felt like forever before my parents got home. The door had a square window at in the top third; whoever it was must have seen me.

When Dad and Mom did get home, I cried and showed them the wood chips on the floor, sobbing my heart out. Dad and Mom were mad and started fighting. They wanted to know where Nancy was, and they were asking me. "I don't know," was all I could say. I was told, "Go to bed!"

I went, crying my eyes out. Listening to the angry voices was the last thing I heard before falling asleep. Nothing was ever said to me, but later my parents were yelling at Nancy, and she said, "I don't care. It's not my job to look out for Emily." The next night my parents went out, I was alone with Nancy, and she was mad at me for telling on her. I had gotten her into trouble. I was to shut my mouth if I knew what was good for me. Nancy hated me for telling on her. I learned at a very early age that I had better be prepared.

The house was mostly empty, both Evan and Nancy would be gone once Mom and Dad left for the night. I would be alone, standing on our front lawn, looking up at the stars coming into the night sky. I loved looking up at the stars. Then I would go into the house and start locking all the doors and checking all the windows. The locking of doors would turn out to be something I would do for the better part of my life.

CHAPTER 22:
IT IS WHAT IT IS

I was home alone. The TV was on, the volume down real low, and the same light was on in the corner. Mom didn't move things around in our house. I was getting accustomed to being alone. I didn't know where everyone was, but I was guessing Evan and Nancy were off with friends. Things didn't happen every night; sometimes I could go to bed, but other times Evan would have a party or Nancy would come home to change.

This one night, I heard the basement door open. The door has a distinctive creaking sound. I call out, "Evan, is that you?" I was mad at myself because I must have forgotten to lock the basement door. I always forget things.

"Evan?" I hoped that it would be him, but no one answers.

Not a sound. I know I heard the basement door. I sat bolt upright on the sofa. Every nerve in my body was on alert! "Evan?" I called once more because it could be Evan playing a joke on me. He had done that before, but he wouldn't leave me hanging. Still no answer.

Oh no. Confronted by this unsettling event again, tears wanted to come to my eyes. "No, not again, please. Why me?" I couldn't go to bed wondering if someone was in the basement, and I knew I'd heard the basement door. I waited to see if someone would be coming up the stairs and curled myself up in a ball on the sofa. I waited and waited, but no one came. I cried, and my heart broke. *Please, no. Now I'll have to go down the stairs and see if someone is there.* It never occurred to me to ask for help, because if I were wrong, my sister would get into trouble for not staying to babysit me. My parents wouldn't be home so I couldn't make her mad at me. She was the closest I had to a friend.

"Why is no one home? Come home, someone. Please come home." I cried and talked to myself. I was not as little as I had been the first time, but I was paralyzed with fear, and I knew that I would have to go down into the basement by myself. I couldn't move. *Oh, please, someone come home. Please help me!*

The problem I feared was once I was at the bottom of the basement stairs I'd have to reach my hand out into the darkness, across the sliding door opening to turn on the basement light. I couldn't stop myself from wondering if someone would grab my arm when I reached out.

I got up off the sofa, my stomach hurting, crying and looking down at the stairs. Only darkness. Not a sound came from the basement. I sobbed and I begged, but no one came home. I was pacing quietly back and forth, looking down into the darkness again. No, please, no. Tears poured from my eyes! It took me some time to work up the nerve to start down those stairs. I got about halfway down and ran less than quietly back up the stairs, screaming and crying. I sat at the top of the stairs, staring into the darkness below, wondering, *Why me?* "Please, please someone come home. Someone please help me," I whispered so that I wouldn't feel so alone.

I didn't know what made me brave enough, but I made it down those stairs, got the light on, and screamed all the way back up to the top again. I was happy that I didn't get grabbed by some unknown hand and snatched away into the darkness. I kept telling myself that I had made it. This feeling of "I made it" was short-lived as I still had to look in the basement. The lights were on, and no one grabbed my hand. So down the stairs I went again, quietly, step by step until I reached the bottom. I very cautiously stepped out onto the basement floor, looking back and forth, and there it was the basement door, wide open! My mind sunk with awareness. Someone indeed had opened the door, but who? Thankfully, the basement was an open design. Only the laundry room and this door were wide open. I could see that no one was there. I ran across the room, slamming the door loudly. I locked it with trembling hands. I was shaking so hard I could hardly walk.

I was crying loudly, with deep sobs, as I could now let my fears out. Drained, I still worried, *Where have the bad guys gone? Are they waiting until I go to sleep?* I told no one, because who could I tell? I just felt trapped in a spot where I could not speak.

* * *

I wish that I could give an age along with this story, but not having birthday acknowledgements, plus the huge issue of my sister's birthday made it even harder to even think about ages. I still have troubles with birthdays. I like giving gifts early or whenever I find the right gift. The day of birthdays mean nothing to me. I do not get hung up on dates like Christmas. As far as that goes, I can celebrate it anytime in December.

CHAPTER 23: BABYSITTING

I was older now, eleven. Not even a year had passed since the basement door event, and I was now babysitting across the street. I could see either Evan or Nancy come home for something or another, watching from the window of our neighbour's house where I babysat. It would really upset me because I didn't know if they locked the doors when they left. Both Evan and Nancy were careless that way.

I needed a chair to stand on so I could reach into the baby's crib as I was still pretty tiny and so very skinny. My hands were shaking as I was afraid of those giant diaper pins and I talked baby talk and the baby was happy. I would place my hand inside the diaper to protect the baby's skin, and sometimes I would stab myself in the hand because it was hard to push those big pins through the cloth. I was really nervous. I sure didn't want to hurt the baby.

There were three children in the house. One had a mental disability. He was almost as tall as I was. Sometimes he would give me some real troubles. I quickly learned how to do things with him that were fun, like singing a song or picking up a toy and laughing at it. He was okay with me. I babysat for this family for years about three, or four nights a week. Mom would tell me what nights I would be babysitting. I never talked back. I just did as I was told. Once home, my money went to Mom. I did try to hide it in my bedroom, but she always found it. Sometimes I would hide some money outside so that I could buy candy bar at the store. I would buy Mom a chocolate bar too because this always made her happy.

 I was such a troubled person. My memory was still hit and miss, I still couldn't say some words correctly, and spelling was my fear. I felt so different from all the other kids, so I needed Mom on my side. I was so lost I stayed close to home. Mom would say, "I don't understand why the teachers can't get through to you because I think you're smart enough." Mom didn't like teachers. They didn't know how to reach me. I didn't trust teachers either. Life was easier if you didn't argue with Mom. My sister almost became an outcast. Because of all her questions, she spent very little time at home as a teenager.

CHAPTER 25: THE DOOR

Once I was older and had been babysitting for a year or so, I was given a key for the downstairs door for when my job was over. I had asked Dad to please change the outside light bulb because it was so dark at night and I couldn't see to use the key, but I guess he kept forgetting. Night after night I would struggle in the dark to get the key in the lock and quickly get inside. Once safe inside the house, it was dark, but I could move around in the dark pretty good and knew where the light switches were. It was quiet, and I would be listening for any strange sounds coming from inside or outside the house.

One warm summer night, I was leaving from my babysitting job. It was very pleasant out I remember feeling like that, pleasant. My job was over and I could go home to bed. I was tired and proud to help bring in some money for the house. I was walking in the dark of the trees coming up to the path leading to our house. A man wearing a black jacket with a pouch in the front for his hands and the hood up covering his head came walking out from the shadows by the carport at the other side.

"What?" I stopped dead in my tracks. My guess is that he was a teenager; he was kind of skinny.

He walked right up to the front of the house and stopped to look inside the living room window between the curtains, putting his hands up to see in. Next, he walked up to the front door. I could see this person was trying the door handle. Holding my breath in disbelief, I backed farther into the shadows. *I haven't been seen.* Never taking my eyes off this person, I backed into a full-grown tree and bumped into the trunk, making a small gasp, and sunk down until I was sitting on the ground. My heart was pounding so hard I thought for sure I would be heard.

Next, the man went down the stairs and around the corner into the darkness, heading for the basement door and disappearing from my view. My eyes grew large and my mouth went dry. I was having trouble breathing. I could feel tears wants to drop. This was the same basement door I had just been heading for a moment earlier. What if he had come around to the basement door while I was struggling to get the key into the lock? My eyes strained to see just where he was, this stranger.

I could hear nothing, and I could see nothing. Anxiety filled me. Where did he go? I felt my cheeks flush hot. I felt shattered inside. Where was he now? I had so many feelings inside me that I couldn't just pick one. I wondered if this person would be back, walking right past me. Oddly enough, I never moved. Not a muscle. I was frozen, sitting and waiting. I didn't have any idea how long I sat there.

Looking back at the house in which I was babysitting, I saw that all their lights were out. They had gone to bed. I didn't want to step out into the light of the street. What I wanted to do was, you know, go to bed! I was alone, listening to the pounding of my own heart. Time was gone. I did wonder if this person was inside the house. Was the back door locked? I didn't cry this time. I didn't think I had it in me to cry.

CHAPTER 26: WINTER

We would all go for a long, long drive to find just the right Christmas tree for Mom. She liked the look of a ponderosa pine tree. Our Christmas tree always had blue lights. The outside lights Dad put up had lots of colours. Mom liked dark colours. Dad even painted our house dark chocolate brown. My bedroom dresser was painted dark chocolate brown. Mom liked her chocolate brown colours, almost black, maybe because she liked chocolate bars. I liked the smell of the tree in the house, and the blue lights did look pretty nice.

Dad would take the garden hose when the weather changed to freezing and water down our front lawn until it was a sheet of ice so we could ice skate on it. I watched by the big living room window as I was too young and too cold. I was always cold. Our outdoor rink always looked like fun. I was always cold in the winter, placing a blanket over the heat vent on the floor. The blanket would blow up into a bubble and warm me right up. Later, I learned that I had low blood pressure and was told this could explain my coldness.

Dad built a great big bobsled that lots of the neighbour kids would enjoy playing on. Our house was at the top of a hill, so it was a perfect starting place for a fast ride down. I did get to ride on this a few times before Dad sent me into the house. Dad was having fun with all the other kids, so into the house I went. It was a fun ride. It would slide another block after the hill, very thrilling. Mom didn't come outside for any of these things, but she always made us hot chocolate. Yup, Mom liked her chocolate.

We would get groups together and walk down to the swamp for a night of ice skating. The swamp was up behind the elementary school. Dad would build a campfire to keep us warm I didn't think I ever left that fire as all I really remember about doing this was freezing.

I did, however, in the summertime spend a lot of time going back and forth to the swamp because of the tadpoles and then frogs. I could play alone around in the water for hours until older kids started hanging out there and they scared me, so it was back to my little creek that came out of nowhere out behind our house.

CHAPTER 27: PARTY? WHAT PARTY?

I do remember a few parties happened at our house, mostly Evan's parties. If Nancy had any I just didn't remember. This was summertime. Evan and his friends were drinking on our front lawn, making noise and goofing around. This caused a problem for our new neighbour lady, Mrs. Jones. Her house was right across the street from us. When she saw the goings-on at our house, she phoned my parents the very next day.

I got home from school to very unhappy parents. I put my head down and answered nothing. I wasn't going to talk even if I was going to get a spanking. I knew full well that I couldn't say anything. Oh sure, Dad and Mom were really mad now, and they wanted to know, but nothing would come of this other than me making both my brother and sister mad at me for telling on them. My parents weren't home a lot, so it was important for me to stay on good terms with them.

"Did Evan have a party here last night? What was going on here? Where was Nancy? The neighbours said there was a party going on here last night. Was there?" Both Dad and Mom were firing questions at me.

Oh, they sure tried to get me to talk, but I knew if I talked Evan and Nancy would be really mad at me, so I said nothing. Just kept my head down and struggled not to cry, mumbling "I don't know," over and over. This was a trap I didn't want to be in. Then my mom said the most disconcerting thing a little girl could ever hear in a serious tone. "Mrs. Jones said she was going to call Social Services and have you taken away!"

My body went cold, w*hat? Why me?* I was trying to fight the tears that wanted to come to my eyes, and my stomach was starting to twist up. This one-sided argument with both my Dad and Mom yelling at me ended when Dad said, "Emily doesn't know anything. Get out of here."

I got shoved away, and I went as fast as I could to my little creek to hide. I didn't know what I had done, but I was more than thrilled to get away from them as fast as possible. Who are these Social Services people? Why do they want me? Where are they going to take me? I was quite terrified. The time I spent worrying about these Social Services people consumed me. I waited for dark before I came home that night and became very watchful around new people. I decided I would need good hiding spots and now everywhere.

CHAPTER 28: WHEN CHRISTMAS CHANGED

Grandma and Grandpa with the big cherry tree came over to our house almost every Christmas. We were not to open any gifts until they were with us. We did get one gift the night before: pyjamas, so when we woke up in the morning we would look good. It was great going to bed with new pyjamas, and I passed this tradition on to my children years later. Our stockings were the one thing we could have in the morning while we waited for our grandparents to arrive. Evan was the one who came into my room with my stocking. He was always good about this, putting a smile on my face before he would leave. We stayed in our rooms separately while we waited for Dad to get back.

This one Christmas morning, our grandparents went to another family member's place. Nancy, a shy young teenager, was opening her gift from Mom. She tore off the wrapping paper in excitement and then jumped up from the sofa screaming and crying. *What?* She raced from the living room crying, clearly heartbroken. I looked into the box that she had dropped, which was laying on the floor and was puzzled, not understanding what had happened. It just looked like some sort of white fuzzy stuff. Evan seemed to know what it was everyone was laughing at. I guess me too, but I was really puzzled.

It would be years before I found out what had happened. No one explained what had happened and I didn't ask. What could it have been from Mom that would make Nancy leave crying?

The Christmas that I got to cry was when I had this big box under the tree. I was so excited that I didn't want to touch it, didn't want to spoil my own surprise. But I sure wondered what it could be. I didn't know how many days I waited for Christmas to come, but it seemed a long time. On Christmas Day I sat on the floor with this big pretty wrapped gift in front of me. I tore away the paper, opened it up, and reached all around inside lots of rolled-up paper. Nothing. It was empty. Just crunched paper. Funny for the whole family but me. My guess was it was just my turn to cry. It was okay. Gave Nancy a break. I always thought she could use one.

To this very day, I have mixed emotions about Christmas. For me, it's the dinner because it was always good. Grandma and Grandpa with the big cherry tree came for Christmas dinner, and this would be really good because Grandma was a really good cook. It was friendly at the table, not crazy friendly, but no dead silences either. Just polite chitter-chatter. Mom would cook Brussels sprouts with our turkey dinner. I liked them. The only time we got to eat them was at Christmas time. Same goes for that orange that came from the box. One orange in your stocking Christmas morning. This was the only meal I remember that none of us ever had to stay sitting at the table because it was a great dinner. Everyone enjoyed it because Grandma had helped.

CHAPTER 29: HIGH SCHOOL

High school was an unbelievable struggle for me, as was my home life. I knew I was not like the other kids. I didn't want anyone to know I was so different, with this off-balance, constant worrying emotion, as if I alone had walked through some abstract door. I continued to stay close to home because at least my family understood me. Plus, I had some great places to hide to be by myself. I could never quite put my fingers on the many whys in my life. It was like I would just start to get it and then it would change. And then there were those awful nightmares.

These nightmares changed, from walls crushing down on me and that horrible sound of rubber so very hard-pressed I felt sick but couldn't move ... to a nightmare of two people, a lady and a little girl, both wearing dresses, walking down a sidewalk. Everything was going good; they are laughing and smiling until they turned a corner onto another street. Everything looked fine, but I could feel an awful dread and terror pouring over my body. Everything went dark like a cloud covering the sun. I wanted to stop them, but I couldn't move, and I couldn't talk. All I was my eyeball.

Down the street they walked. The sky got so dark, but they didn't seem to see this. I searched around with my eyes, wondering why I was so afraid. What was it? Then I spied a dark shadow, standing in a window watching them. I want to scream to them, but I had no voice. Nothing came out. *Please*, I was yelling inside my head, *please look out*. They keep walking, hand and hand, talking. They were not sensing what I was and I couldn't make them hear me.

I would wake up, my heart pounding so hard in my chest, lying under my blanket, telling myself it was just another nightmare. That awful feeling of terror was slow to let me go. *Please stop, please stop giving me nightmares*. I would cry myself back to sleep.

The teachers in high school knew that I was not understanding things. I got sent to the school counsellor, and he did tests on me and were very surprised that I had a pretty high IQ, which I understood meant I could think outside the box. Mr. Nicole said he couldn't understand why I was having such a hard time with my memory. I quite liked Mr. Nicole. He talked about his part-time job, search and rescue. I liked that he felt I wasn't a lost cause and didn't call me stupid and seem to think I wasn't a waste of time. He was nice to me. I was painfully aware I was different, watching the other kids gather and talking a fascinating new language with laughter, not a worry in the world. I would try to pick up a new word or two and work them over in my head on the long walk uphill to home.

I was very thin and still had a dislike for food because it tasted so bad; not the meat but the veggies. I was conscious that I was not like the other kids in ways I just didn't understand. They could spell no problem and could remember things that I struggled with all the time. I was gangly and awkward with fuzzy blonde hair and blue eyes. Pale, thin, and scrawny was what I was called. However, some said I had spunk! I think this was because I tried so hard to be funny.

New names or words I would have to practice, saying them by myself over and over. Sometimes this helped, but sometimes not. *Why can I not hold a train of thought like my friends do? What's wrong with me?* The sadness grew inside of me. With speech difficulties, it's like from my brain to my tongue things get lost! Actually, I was told this by my counsellor, Mr. Nicole. Having a bad memory was really tough. I was unable to relax. It was hard for me to settle down. Words were not my friends, which is odd because here I am struggling with words and writing this.

My life was full of extremes, between hopes and fears. I grew accustomed to life and its misery, always watching out for Social Services people who wanted to take me away. I never told anyone about them. I didn't know why I held these secrets. It would seem to me that I had no voice when it came to the heart of my troubles: falling short by the school standards and having these strange nightmares.

The walls crushing down on intense rubber changed to other types of nightmares. One day I took the chance, and asked my friends, "Do you ever have nightmares?" They shared some stories of their own. So they too had them. This came as quite a relief. Maybe I was not so different after all.

CHAPTER 30: EXCELLENT HIDING SPOTS

The house was mostly empty. Both Evan and Nancy were much older and getting on with their lives, both in relationships, and my brother at home but not for much longer. I was alone, standing outside, looking up at the darkening sky, waiting to see the stars. I liked being alone. I figured this was my life. The doors were almost all locked, but the front door was waiting for me to come inside. I became pretty darn good at this. Always afraid to make a mistake, I became extremely cautious, or so I thought!

I had learned to suppress the fears. I couldn't tell anyone, so I'll have to be careful. I knew I was very much alone, isolated. No one understood me. I was broken in a way that I just didn't understand. It really made me sad that I didn't fit in with any of my friends, as I still struggled to say some words. Panic and anxiousness stayed for the long haul. I just didn't know what I had been doing wrong. I felt I should be doing something, but what? Not knowing what a Social Services person was left me with some very deep wounds.

I spent a lot of time looking for good hiding spots, and I had them everywhere. I was super tiny, so I could squeeze into just about anything—the broom closet or in the back of one of our kitchen cupboards, but the very best spot was under the house. No one knew that Nancy would hide under there, either. I was happiest under our house and would play cards there.

Another thing I started to do at night was to watch horror movies. Lots and lots of horror movies. I wanted and needed to learn what they did on TV when the bad guys showed up. I guess what I should be saying was what "not" to do, as it seems they always get themselves killed in these movies. I did have home advantages and could move around in the dark pretty darn good, so I felt I was almost ready for the world now.

Even at school, I had some great hiding spots, under the stage in the gym. They had these big sliding drawers for the gym mats. If I needed to, I could hide under there or in the supply room in between classes. It wasn't the best place, but worked in a pinch. The janitor's room with the big strange-looking furnace worked, but the large auditorium was the best place ever. I would skip classes, looking for good hiding spots. That way no one would catch me looking. I found this doorway with stairs going up to the top. There were boardwalks. I was fascinated right away! Feeling like I was now comfortable with the way my life was going, I was prepared! The auditorium was super. Up there I could watch shows going on or bands playing. No one ever knew I was up there. Perfect, right?

CHAPTER 31: LONG WEEKEND

We had gone to visit with Mom's parents. I wondered how Mom could visit with Grandpa because of her childhood with him. Mom hugged her dad, and I guess it was a long time ago and she had forgiven him, so this was confusing for me. My cousin Betty was there. She was the same age as me, thirteen—well just about. It was Dad and Mom and me, and it was a long drive for this long weekend to visit Mom's family. I did like watching out the window, seeing how the trees and hillsides changed and seeing the many different flowers. We didn't get there until nighttime. They had placed signs on the dirt road close to their home. The headlights of our car would shine on them, saying that we were almost there. I found this all to be very fun and exciting when our headlights would find another sign in the dark. The very next morning, Betty and I went biking riding all over the place as she had two bikes! When we got tired, we would stop and go swimming in the river. We talked forever. She was really smart about country life, and I just couldn't get enough.

We did some hiking in the bushes and trees, then found some apples on a tree out in a huge field, so we ate some of these. Betty said we must watch out for black bears as they liked apples too! It was so freeing. We giggled and laughed. We didn't see much of the rest of the family because Betty and I were having so much fun.

At dinner time, the whole family and the neighbours got together, and there was this fellow who took a shine to me when we all sat down to eat. He was older by a few years and he was being nice to me, talking with me and asking me questions. I didn't really understand why and this made me very uncomfortable. I did my best to stay away from him, not that he was doing anything wrong, you understand. I just didn't know anything at all about this guy stuff and was having so much fun with Betty, the most fun I think I'd ever had with a friend, and I wasn't worried about hiding places. When the weekend came to an end, I was sad because I'd miss Betty and all this freedom we had together. I promised her that I would write her.

What a great time. I hoped that we would be seeing each other again soon. We had gotten into our car, saying our goodbyes. The long weekend was over. Heading for home, I couldn't have been happier, sitting in the back seat of our car, waving until I couldn't see them anymore. I had a smile on my face that just wouldn't quit.

Once out of sight from the relatives and friends, Mom turned around in the front seat to look at me. She was really mad. My eyes popped open. The look on her face shocked me and my heart sank. I was quite lost as to what I had done.

In a very flat angry voice, Mom said, "Who do you think you are? That man liked you! Do you think this is ever going to happen for you again?"

Stunned, I was struck with fear. I had no idea what she was talking about. Sitting up against the door as close as I could get, I wished I could disappear. *Who do I think I am? What did this mean?* I was baffled. My happy feelings abruptly changed. I felt like I was suffocating in a darkness that's worming its way deep inside of me. I could feel the tears, but I was afraid to cry. I mean, I was really clueless as to what she was saying. What I knew was I'd done something to make her really mad! Dad must have done something because Mom looked sharply at him and turned around again sitting back in her seat, nothing more was said. A creepy silence.

I really didn't understand but could feel she was mad. *Who do I think I am?* I stared out the car window, thinking hard, the scenery passing by without me seeing a thing. I was empty of all feelings and stuck in the car now for hours. *That man liked me? What was it Mom was saying and why was she so mad? What should I have been doing? What's wrong with me? What have I done?* My mind was spinning.

Yet I was to do something. For the life of me, I had no idea what it was. When we got home, something had changed. I no longer felt welcome or less welcome than before. Dad once in a while played a card game with me, and we did have some good laughs together, but Mom I think I was to grow up and get out of the house soon.

So this long car ride back home with Mom saying, "Who do you think you are? That man liked you," was a huge turning point. I was crushed and sick with worry, but I dared not cry. Later in the week, Mom calmed down. She did tell me that men have needs and I would understand this later in life. *Men have needs?*

CHAPTER 32: WHAT IS WRONG WITH HER?

How could my life get any worse? I was now going into grade 9. I wasn't developing fast enough as a woman—no boobs. Mom took me to the doctors to find out what was wrong with me and I didn't know that we were going to the doctors until we were there. I just sat in his office, hopelessly lost and hurt, because once again something was terribly wrong with me. My mom talked about me like I was not even in the room with the doctor. "She is not developing as a woman. Is there something that can be done? What is wrong with her?"

My head was down. I did not look at anyone and felt sick and sad at the same time. The doctor said there was nothing wrong, that some girls grow faster and some girls grow slower. He tried to reassure her that I was fine, but Mom changed her questions. "She hasn't started her menstrual cycle yet. What's wrong with her?"

Again I heard the doctor reassure Mom that I was fine, and when I was leaving, he put a hand on my shoulder and smiled. We left the doctor's office with my mom saying, "He's not a very good doctor. He should have tried to do something to help you develop as a woman."

It was the following summer before I had my first menstrual cycle. We were camping with their friends. When I told my mom, she was off to tell the other ladies. The school had put out a book on this stuff and Mom had come into my room and said I should read it later. I felt creeped out because it wasn't like Mom to do this, come in my room and talk with me. Thank goodness I had a girlfriend who told me some of what she knew about this messy stuff. To my surprise, I was going to have this happen to me every month.

CHAPTER 33: NANCY'S BOYFRIEND

Evan had a girlfriend that he liked very much. She seemed very nice, but I didn't see a lot of them. Nancy also had a boyfriend, and she seemed way happier. Plus she got a job too!

Nancy had met a guy in high school and had started dating. Mom was happy about this but didn't care for them hanging out alone in our basement. My parents would give me a few coins if I would go downstairs and bug her with her date. Barry, her date, would give me a dollar to get lost. I would head right out the basement door to the candy store. This happened more than once. I thought life was great again and that sometimes secrets were incredibly good. I would walk well over a mile to the corner store. Sometimes both Nancy and Barry would hang out at the house with me in the nighttime when I was alone. This was great fun. Barry could always make us laugh, and he really liked that our Mom had told us girls that men have needs. I still didn't understand, but my sister did. They would laugh together about this, and I was just happy that someone was at home. On the plus side, I could go to bed and sleep—no nightmares. Barry was a great guy, and my sister and I started to get along much better now that she seemed happy. We didn't ever talk about the strange family life we had because from what I know now this takes a very long time to figure out. Nancy would bring up something like not being allowed into the house when she was little and going to the bathroom outside. Nancy struggled with Dad a lot too, he would call her meathead, and she would make a face that looked hurt. I felt the same!

CHAPTER 34:
TOYS

Evan had been working and had graduated from grade 12. No one said a thing about that. No party, not even a card or a "Good for you, son." He had graduated completely unnoticed. I didn't have any idea what graduation from high school meant. I did ask Mom, "What happens after graduation?" Mom said, "He goes out and gets a job." But Evan had had a job for years. I just didn't understand.

Nancy had her job, and I have been the babysitter for the lady across the street. All of us kids had jobs. I didn't know how this all worked, but Mom took all my money from babysitting. I hid some of my babysitting money outside; it took me a year or two to figure this out, and the rest I put in my bedroom and Mom would take that.

I had saved up some money outside to buy a small TV for my bedroom, and I bought one from an uncle. It came into the house, and I was pretty excited, but Dad took the TV and put it in their bedroom, I never did get to use my TV I bought. I didn't mind. It hurt a little, and I didn't know what to do so if this made them happy I guess I liked that I had made my parents happy.

Later after the TV, I saved hidden money up for a good sleeping bag because we did a lot of camping and I didn't like waking up cold in the mornings; I wanted a good warm sleeping bag. That money was taken away by Mom because we needed food in the house first, again I didn't mind because if Mom was happy then I was happy. So I didn't get a sleeping bag but I did get an extra blanket.

Any toys given to us or toys that I got for myself would just disappear, and I knew better than to ask where they went because that was just how life was. One day you had some toy and before you knew it was gone. Mom was not a person that you could talk with. After watching my sister struggle trying to make headway, only to wind up sad and hurt, I learned to just take what was dished out and stayed as far away as I could.

However, I did buy myself this little toy rubber bouncy mouse. It was blue, and I loved it. A girlfriend and I took the bus way across town to a place I had never been before. It was called a mall. We were so far from home it took one bus transfer to get there. If I got lost from my girlfriend, I would never make it back home. That's where I bought this mouse, in this store that had it seemed to me everything a kid would love. Another girlfriend had shown me how to thread a needle and sew. Her family was so nice, and I really liked being there. I would hang out there whenever I could and tried to make clothes for this great little toy mouse. I loved it and secretly played with this mouse all the time, until one day when I came home Mom said that she had let the neighbour's baby play with it and it was chewed up. I must have forgotten to hide it because I thought I had a good hiding place. One eye was gone, and so was my little blue mouse's tail and ear. I cried when I looked at it. My heart was broken. I sat alone under the house and swore I would never like another toy. Mom never said another thing about it. She walked away like I was foolish for even liking it.

CHAPTER 35: SHE'S A VERY WILFUL GIRL

Nancy was the only one who had to pay rent. Evan didn't have to, and you guessed it, Nancy complained. A lot. Nancy, the fighter, would ask Mom day after day, "Why am I the only one paying rent?" This fight lasted a long time, and again she never did get any real answers.

One day at the bank with Mom, Nancy asked if she could open up a bank account Mom said no. When Mom wasn't looking and was busy doing her own banking, a bank lady came up to Nancy and said, "Come back without your mom, and we will help you open up an account." Nancy had done it. Wow! She opened up her first bank account. I overheard her talking. It was a big secret. I watched everything from a safe distance and thought, *Gee, I would like to open a bank account too! I could save up some of my babysitting money.* So I waited until some time had passed, maybe a year, and I had some money hidden away. I asked Mom if I could open up a bank account. {After all Nancy made it and enough time had passed.} In a very flat tone, Mom said, no I was too young, end of story. I never did ask again. I didn't want to push on this subject because I could tell that Mom was not happy about Nancy opening up a bank account. It would be my sister-in-law and my first husband that would show me how to write cheques, many years later.

Nancy had the nerve to want to buy her first car with the money she had saved. Good for her. Evan had already been through two cars, and he worked to buy them on his own. Evan had his own money, and strangely enough Mom didn't take from him that I know of. Nancy made the big mistake of asking Dad and Mom for help. *What were you thinking? What were you thinking?* Oh, a big fight over this as they made her buy Evan's old car. He wanted to sell it, and it would help him out. I went into my hiding place under the house because Evan was the one child who, from where I stood, was given everything. I wondered about who got the money, but as far as I know it was Evan.

Did this stop Nancy? Oh no, now she wanted to buy a house because she kept on saving her money, even though she had to go to school and pay rent! She even knew which house she wanted to buy. I was proud of her and very much wanted for her to get on with her life. The hope was that one day I could do the same. Dad and Mom said no it would be too much for her to handle. Our parents always wanted to restrict her. I think they didn't want Nancy doing better than Evan because he was the boy. Sadly, she didn't get the house, but she did move out and rented her own place. We didn't go and visit her at her new place, but she did make it out of our house for good. Dad or Mom didn't talk about Nancy. She was gone, and I missed her and her boyfriend very much.

This one day, Nancy had come home to visit, and she told me this much later in life. Nancy said, "When I got to the front door, I just stood there. I didn't know what I should do. Do I knock, or do I just open the door and walk in?" She said she felt like an intruder and stood outside, looking at the front door for a long time.

I didn't ask questions, so I didn't know what she ended up doing to that very day, but it left that same tragic feeling in my body that I could never quite understand. Nancy was engaged to Barry. They had been together since like forever high school. This should have been a happy time, and I think it was in some ways; however, Mom went to Barry's job and chased him, down telling him he shouldn't marry her. "She is a very wilful girl. You are not strong enough to handle her."

Thank goodness he didn't listen to Mom because they have been together some 40 years. In a strange way, I guess Mom was just looking out for Nancy, but I was so glad that she didn't get her way because Nancy found happiness.

CHAPTER 36: LIFE CHANGES

The house was empty, only myself left. Dad and Mom sold the house and bought a business up country and it came with acres of land. Dad wasn't quite ready to retire, so we moved into grandma's basement, my mom's mom. We travelled back and forth to the new business and these beautiful acres. I loved walking around it, plus it had a lake out front. The wildlife was unreal compared to what we had down the coast. Frogs, black bears, and I even heard the scream of a cougar. There were outhouses, trees, and bushes with flowers. Oh yes, and snakes; they were really big!

I met a guy at a get-together. He seemed to be nice, and Mom couldn't have been happier and wanted to know when I was going to get married and have babies? Gosh I was still in grade 9, but until I got married Mom thought that I should be on birth control pills. Jeepers, Mom was in such a hurry. Nancy was pregnant. Life was spinning to fast.

I would take the Greyhound bus up to visit my new boyfriend and his family. He had a large family and dinner time was amazing. So many people sitting at the table and talking like crazy. I was spellbound and had never in my life seen anything like this. It was really fun!

EMILY KNEW

When I came back to Vancouver by bus it was late, midnight or later, and pretty scary on the streets downtown, where Vancouver's bus stop was. Walking down the lonely streets at this hour was scary, and the city bus drivers that I always sat right up front with said how worried they were about me travelling alone at this late an hour, wanted to know if someone would be picking me up at my stop. I would tell them that I didn't live that far away from my stop. It was only a few blocks. I thought, *How nice of them, but I can hide at the drop of a hat.* I was followed once and gave whoever it was the slip. I felt quite cocky that way. I was used to taking care of myself by now. My parents never once worried about me nor did they ever pick me up. I thought, *why should these bus drivers worry? This seems pretty silly of them.* I thought of myself as being pretty tough.

Nancy, however, did not feel the same way. Gosh, my sister, she questioned everything, it seemed to me. "Why don't you ever come and watch me in track and field, like other parents do? Why are you never there to give me a ride home?" It would be a fight. I would go under the house; it was quieter down there. "Why can't Dad give me a ride in the mornings he goes right by my school?" I didn't hear how it ended, but would get really quiet after all was said and done.

My sister got married. Nancy had to fight Mom for a date and time for her wedding. Dad wasn't happy about giving up his schedule for her, but he did. Then my brother got married. Both my brother and my sister, in my eyes, had found true happiness, and I was so glad for them. The pressure was on me now, and Mom found out Dad had had an affair and oh how I wanted to not be there in the house with them.

CHAPTER 37: MARRIAGE AND BABIES

I got married to my new boyfriend because Mom said I was ready and it was time for me to move on. I was engaged at seventeen and married that same year. I felt pretty good, but it sure upset other people. I didn't understand because Mom had wanted me dating at 13. I had held out for as long as I could. He was a nice guy, and for a while things were pretty good.

There was this wedding shower that the family had for me. It was nice of them to do this, and I didn't really understand what was happening, but I knew that this was what Mom had been waiting for. After this wedding shower, everyone in the family was mad at me because I didn't send out thank you cards. I was hurt and didn't understand what these cards were all about, and even Mom was mad at me for not doing this.

My wedding went just how Mom wanted it. She picked out the date and time, as well as who was coming. There were also people that I didn't want at my wedding, but Mom said I had to have them. I wore my sister's dress that had been our aunt's dress. The day of my wedding, my sister-in-law was very kind to me and helped with my make-up as I was not used to doing that yet. Dad gave me away without a word passing between us.

This poor guy I married had no idea that I was such a broken person. I didn't know how to cook, never mind run a house. I had never shopped for food before, nor had I ever written a cheque but my sister-in-law showed how to do this. Thank goodness for her help. I was out of the house and really trying to understand what I was supposed to be doing. I got pregnant right away and so was my sister Nancy at pretty much the same time but her with her second child. My sister and I were doing what we were told to do for as long back as I can remember and that was to have babies.

My husband worked the night shift, and when my time came in the spring for me to have my baby, Dad and Mom came to help me. When my husband came into the hospital to get me, I was a little scared to be alone with my newborn baby girl. She was so small and so sweet. I wanted her to be happy, and I held her close. We got home Dad and Mom were both right there to greet us. My husband jumped out. The car door opened on my side and Mom took hold of the baby, and the three of them started to head for the house. I sat in the car, a bit shocked, as I felt left behind. No one asked how I was at all. I did say something like, "Hey, what about me?" as I swung my legs out of the car. They looked back at me and laughed and just walked away. I tried to make fun of it, but in my heart I felt a little hurt.

It was my first night at home as a new mommy. My husband went to work we said our goodbyes. Dad and Mom were in the cabin beside the house. This was on the land that my parents owned. We were lucky enough to get it. I was now alone getting ready for bed. Daytime was long gone, and all the visiting was over. My little baby girl was sleeping happily, and I was tired. It seemed to be a long day. I was turning off some of the lights, and I heard the front door open.

In walked Mom, to my surprise. So I turned, looking at her. She walked right up to me: not more than a few feet away. Everything in my body stopped. We were looking eye to eye. I didn't know what it was, but I thought it was the look on her face for some reason, and I didn't understand why I was frozen. I think sometimes I was holding my breath. Mom's voice was calm, but there was something about it—it was flat. She wasn't saying anything meanly, but had a strange kind of concern. I stiffened to attention.

"You know," Mom said softly, looking right into my eyes. "Most people lose their first baby, and if you find her dead in the morning, it won't be your fault as these things just happen. So if she is dead in the morning, I want you to know it's not your fault. Okay, goodnight."

And she turned and walked back out. I heard the door close behind her. A thousand fears had woken in me. I stood for a long time in that very spot, trying to breathe. I couldn't think, or I didn't know what to think. Mom had said it so calmly and with a strange kind of concern. She was almost kind about it. I had absolutely no clue of the menace in which I lived. I had this strange sort of amnesia. I found that now I was not so tired, but caught myself putting clean clothes in with the dirty clothes.

I was walking—or maybe it was more like more pacing—around, barely conscious of what I was doing. Reliving the things about my life I'd tried so hard to forget. I never said anything about this to anyone for a good many years and then only to a small group of my friends. I was watching my newborn baby girl sleeping. I wanted to love her, but now I was scared she would break my heart and die. *How will I live if she were to die?* I went into the washroom and threw up. I didn't sleep well, and those awful nightmares came back hard. Getting up and down, checking on my baby, I'd never slept well anyway, always worrying. So this was not a huge change for me.

I sure didn't tell this to my husband because I didn't want him to be as worried as me. At least that's what I think I was doing. This did change some of my nightmares because now I was having nightmares about my baby girl dying. *Why would Mom say this to me? Did she have a baby die?*

Life went on like it does, and I did what I thought I should be doing, learning how to cook and clean, plus do laundry. I had never learned this at home, so it was quite the struggle.

A year or so went by, and I was going to have another baby. We have moved into my husband's parents' house and are buying it. This baby was a boy, and I was happy to have healthy babies, plus a girl and a boy. This time it was my husband's family that came to the hospital, and they were looking at their grandson happily. They talked about him having this person noise or eyes and "Look at his little feet." My husband's mom held my son in her arms and talked to him. I watched her and thought, *I do this too*.

It was nice coming home my house was cleaned up, his family were so very nice. It was also scary because I wondered, *what's next? Where was the blow up?* I found it hard to breathe or relax. They would play card games. I always liked to play card games. It was fun, didn't matter if I won. I was just glad of the fun. My parents and his were so very different. They had lots of children and stayed at home. These kids could talk about anything with their parents. I would sit in awe of all the chatter at the kitchen table. I told my husband that I'd never seen anything like this. He thought I said that because there were so many kids. What I really meant was, *Wow, they are allowed to talk*. I didn't let him know this because he might think I was strange.

CHAPTER 38:
I WAS LOST

Days later, Dad and Mom had stopped by for a coffee. My husband was at work, and I had no idea that they were coming up for a visit. I now had a newborn baby boy in the house. They have yet to see him, but he was sleeping in his crib. We were at the kitchen table, and I had put on the coffee. I myself liked tea. I take up Jenny into my arms, saying to my parents, "I'll be right back, come on Jenny lets wash those sticky hands." I was off to the washroom to wash her little hands. I leave with little Jenny giggling. When I come back around the corner to the kitchen, Dad was standing, looking up the stairs, saying, "What are you doing going through her bedroom? She's an adult now."

I stopped dead in my tracks, putting Jenny down, and Mom came down the stairs. I could see she was really mad that Dad made her leave my bedroom. She never looked my way when she came down the stair and heads right out the front door. The screen-door closed loudly Dad follows, they both just up and left. No goodbyes. No "Sorry we won't be staying for coffee." Nothing. They just left.

I was puzzled and went upstairs to look around my bedroom. *Why would she be in my bedroom? The bed was made. What was it that she was looking for? Why, would Mom be going through my bedroom? Why does she do these strange things? It leaves me feeling off-balance!* I guess I thought I was doing what I was told to do. You know, having babies.

But still my parents were in my life, doing these strange things. All my problems didn't go away. I liked babysitting, and I liked little kids, and I was good at it.

I for some reason couldn't figure out that it was my parents who were causing me to lose myself. My mind just couldn't go there. I didn't know where to turn or how to think it out. Maybe it hurt too much for me to know at that time. I wish I could understand why I'd taken so long to put things together.

This was confusing and upsetting, to say the very least. It took its toll on me, and that night I had a nightmare. It was brutal. I was in bed, and I started to feel warm. It was nice, and I was sinking deeper into the mattress and deeper into a wonderful sleep. I felt the mattress sink beside me like someone had joined me. A shot of adrenalin ran through my body. A paralyzing fear wrapped around me. I so desperately wanted to move, to wake up, but I felt that if I moved this something on the bed beside me, watching, would violently shred me into pieces. This extreme fear pushed me. I was almost hysterical, and a cold sweat broke out on my body. I screamed desperate cries for help, but I know that no one was coming. In the silence, I could now hear the familiar sounds of the house and woke up sharply, sitting up, looking around, and shuddering a sigh of relief. I collapsed on my pillows, telling myself, *it's only a nightmare*.

I stopped eating and couldn't think clearly anymore. I couldn't get the many whys out of my head. I guess something in me broke because my husband said I needed to see a doctor. He saw how thin I had become and I was put into the hospital for almost a week. I didn't want to live anymore. It was just too hard. I didn't understand what was happening to me. I just stopped eating. It didn't bother me to do this. It took a full-length mirror and seeing my flesh hanging off my body to make me start eating again. I had two little children I knew had to get better. It didn't start all of a sudden, these gaps or not gaps, but strange things that kept showing up in my life. I was lost.

Looking back now, there were so many unexplained incidents that I had tried so very hard to shove aside. I felt that I could never relax and when I slept, I slept deeply. I'd started getting dizzy spells and sometimes I would fall to the ground. I had some of these when I was in school, and those darn hit and miss nightmares just wouldn't give me a break. They come about every six to seven months. Now something else was happening to me.

In the daytime, I'd been experiencing severe headaches, and I mean severe. They came when too much was going on in my life. I would be sitting at the table. First, it was my eyesight. I would not feel quite right. Then these little clouds would be floating around the edges of my sight. Bang. I would be down for the count in a dark room and could not move at all. Even sound hurt. It was like someone took a baseball bat and drove it right into the back of my skull. If I moved my head even just a little—dear Lord, the pain—it was a "please kill me now" kind of pain. It was unbelievable pain, and the only thing I could do was lie still and wait until it passed. It seemed to hit me when I had company and I felt stressed. I would be feeling overwhelmed. The next day I would still feel off. It took me some time to get my feet back under me after one of these headaches.

I had talked again with friends about nightmares, and we all get them from time to time, but I can remember them as far back as when Nancy and I shared a bedroom together. The same nightmares of walls crushing down on very intense rubber. This one was recurring, but now I was getting them with a new twist of dark shadows chasing me. My marriage ended, as things were not right. This, you understand, was not his fault because I never told him what was going on in my life or that I was experiencing a persistent sense of impending doom. I guess it would have been better if I talked to him and maybe he could have stopped my parents from being in my life. I never spoke of the things I've been writing about here.

CHAPTER 39: NIGHTMARES, SECRETS, AND LOCKED DOORS

I was getting two or three nightmares in a row on the very same night. I would close my eyes, and I would back in a nightmare. My heart would be pounding, and I would be soaked in sweat, gasping for air, overwhelmed by a feeling of absolute terror, only to lie down and have yet another one. I did finally see the doctor as it got so bad I was given sleeping pills. These nightmares were always a surprise and very unwelcome. The sleeping pills gave me some relief, but I now worried about depending on sleeping pills.

The doctor sent me to a psychiatrist, but this did no good as I just didn't know what I should be telling him. For some reason I didn't understand, I couldn't say anything. Oh, I saw counsellors in school. I didn't understand why I was the way I was and I felt a hurt in my heart that I couldn't explain. I knew that I carried some sort of burden, guilt, or shame and for some reason I was aware and not aware at the very same time. *What's wrong with me? Am I crazy?* I even thought and talked about giving up my children because I was so afraid of screwing them up like me. This frustration caused me to cry if I thought too much about these things. Everyone would know that there was something wrong with me. There's been something wrong with me my whole life. My doctor said at one appointment that time would help make these nightmares go away. I sure hoped he knew what he was talking about. I found if I just kept on moving as fast as I could, maybe this something wouldn't catch me. Once again, life went on and it was just me and my two children for a number of years.

My children were in school and I was visiting with some lady friends, and we were sharing some good laughs. One of the ladies got up to leave. It was early afternoon. The sun was shining. It was a beautiful day. She was saying her goodbyes, and she headed for the front door, reached for the doorknob, and started to laugh. "Emily must be here as the doors are locked."

Everyone started to laugh and look at me because it's common knowledge for them. They all knew that this was something that I did all the time, but I was unaware I was doing this. My insides were profoundly affected as my guts twisted up tight. I felt off-balance by this news. I laughed with my friends because here it was again there was something wrong with me. I carried an impenetrable secret so obscure that I was traumatized. It was like some part of my mind knew this was very real that I was doing this, but it was irrational, and I struggled to understand the whys. I was doing something, and I had no memory of what I was doing. *Why am I locking doors?* I had pushed all memories of my past away and had no idea why I was locking doors. I shoved this new thought aside and laughed with my friends, but it somehow tickled around the edges of my mind. These pieces of my past, these shifting images kept racing on.

There was something not quite right about me. I was tormented. It was like a slap in the face so sudden, with some shard of memory unexpectedly surfacing just to remind me that I was broken. *What is it that I can't fully retrieve? I live with some dark shadow that I can barely see.* I think I feared the answer and what it could reveal. I had a moment of pure panic. I went home from what should have been a wonderful day with friends, but instead I went home and worry. *What is wrong with me?*

My world was slowly falling apart, and I was so afraid of being a burden to my friends. They said the world was full of mystery. Well, an even bigger mystery lived inside of me. Something deep and forbidden. I carried some sort of unmentionable secret, but I feared using my voice. Why, this door locking thing, this would overwhelm me now for weeks. How could it be that I was doing this and how could everyone but me, know I was doing this? Do I have a form of amnesia? Was there some unremembered life haunting me? I have no idea what it was, but it was slowly killing me from the inside out. I was trapped in a whirlwind and life just kept moving on. I was doing all the right things for the outside world to see: smiling, talking, doing some shopping, blindly going about my tasks. The effort this took was wearing and absolutely isolating.

I still managed to have a life, and there were good moments that I have shared with people, but I carried a heartache and had no idea how to deal with it. I continued to visit with my Dad and Mom because at the very least they knew me and they knew about my lifelong problems. We did have good times together, but I always felt edgy around them. I really wanted to please my parents, and I would do just about anything or give up anything of my own if it would have helped make them happy. Mom could say things like she liked the colour of my hair with the shirt I was wearing. That would make me smile. I would think it was a start for us getting closer. We could sit and have a drink on her deck and talk about some flower growing in the yard. We would be almost normal, but the next visit everything changed. Mom would talk about Evan like he was the only person in the world. "Evan's lost weight," or "Evan's looking great," or "Evan just sold something and is making big money," or Evan took them somewhere. Evan, Evan, Evan. Nothing you could say didn't somehow come back to Evan.

One day, out of the blue Mom told me that she used to give us kids gravel pills, travel sickness pills, to make us sleep when we were little. I had no idea why she had just out of the blue told me this. It was that same calm voice that she always used when she wanted me to listen. I never asked her questions. I think I feared her answers, but for some reason I couldn't explain I was overwhelmed by this and it made me feel shaky-edgy. I did two things. I started making things funny or I froze and didn't know how to feel. One thing I never did was tell anyone. I thought, *why would anyone care about these silly little things?* I for some reason lost my voice and to stay sane I would shut it out of my mind, pushing it back. *Please don't think. Please don't think of anything terrible. It doesn't mean anything.*

Even when Mom and I were having a good time I fought to repress these feelings. I thought it was because I sensed that she was going to say something and she did but never when you were ready. *It was silly or seemed unimportant, or was it? Why did she tell me this?* "Evan won't look at any of his baby pictures." *What why are you telling me this? I don't look at my baby pictures, either. Does this mean something?* My mind holds these silly comments, and they roll around and around. Where do I put this? It was from out of the blue when Mom said them, but it felt important somehow. It wasn't like I could go crying to a girlfriend and say, "Evan won't look at his baby pictures" or "Mom said she gave us kids Gravel sickness pills to make us sleep."

Frankly, who cared? That was a long time ago, but these things had some effect on me and they won't go away. I experienced great stress. I felt lost and uncomfortable. I could not see my situation and I saw no solutions, nor did I remember at this time locking doors from my childhood. These are part flashbacks and part something else. Which brought me back to the idea that there was something wrong with me. Why couldn't I let it go?

Mom talked about my brother Evan mostly when I was feeling down. She would talk endlessly about my brother's accomplishments and or even his struggles; nothing else in the world mattered more than Evan. It got to be so much I would almost choke when I heard her start to use his name.

I wondered if she even knew that she had daughters. I didn't hear Mom talk about Nancy. She had made a life for herself and her family, and we didn't see a lot of each other for some time. Once in a while Nancy and I talked on the phone. We would keep things pretty light and short. Nothing that could hurt. Small talk. We wondered if Mom only loved us as out of obligation until we were needed for something. When Mom talked about us girls she even called us "the daughters." It was "the daughters" this or "the daughters" that. When you least expected it, she would do something nice, and I would be mad at myself for thinking the way I did. Oh the guilt! Nancy and I would say, "Well, it's not like kids come with instructions," as we both had children too. Maybe there were lots of things from Mom's past that made her the way she was. We tried hard to be understanding.

I married again, but it didn't make it but two years. We met, and Phil was so good at doing things with me and my children. I thought maybe it could work. He wouldn't take just me out to dinner, but my kids too. That was a first for me to meet someone like that, and he could sing. Mom said that I should marry Phil because he would help me with my children. Mom liked Phil right away. He had said, "What a good-looking lady you are and what great-looking legs." When I introduced him to my mother, she giggled. I was not finding a lot of men who wanted a woman with two children, and Phil even took me and my two kids swimming at the town pool. I had been alone a long time, six years, and I thought maybe I had found someone who could help me with my family. It was not a good marriage, but I sure wished it could have been. I so wanted it to be. I later heard my mother saying, "I don't know why she married him."

I found myself alone again, but this time other people are now noticing that there was something not right about me. The second marriage felt hard to let go of because now it wasn't just him but me. Now my children were feeling the effects of my mistakes, and I knew I had to stop spinning out of control and stay in a relationship. Whatever it was that sending me for a loop, I had to stop letting things get to me and get on with my life, and that's what I'd thought I was doing.

There was this guy who said he really liked me, so this became a fast getting together, and marriage number three. I learned a lot from the many years we were together. My parents didn't like him all that much, and that was good by me. He had his role in my life and, what can I say? My parents sort of dropped out of my life for a while. It worked for me a long time. My parents didn't visit with me much. Perfect.

CHAPTER 40: MOM'S BLUE DRESS

This blue dress was stunning on Mom. She was a beautiful-looking woman and had always taken care of her looks. I remember her wearing this blue dress, I believe it was New Year's. It flowed softly as she walked.

Many years later, my parents stopped in for a visit and I got a sewing machine from Mom and the beautiful blue dress. I was thrilled. We have a wonderful time together. It was a short surprise visit and I felt super about this. We played card games after dinner and sat talking with other people. Things were good and I started to relax, smiling.

After my parents left, I excitedly opened the bag with this beautiful blue dress because I wanted to try it on. I stripped down to my bra and panties. Over my head it went. It had been cut open under the arms and couldn't be fixed. *What? Why would she give this to me?* There came that strange feeling I knew so well. Now I looked over at the sewing machine and wondered. Mom said it needed something but that it was just like new. Phil takes the sewing machine in for me to get it fixed and I say nothing about the blue dress.

A week later, we hear this sewing machine was so broken that it couldn't be fixed. My heart sank. I didn't have an answer and I'd never ask for an answer. I phoned to talk with my sister Nancy about the sewing machine Mom gave me and that it was broken. Nancy said that Mom gave her bags full of strange clothes that would almost fall apart they were so old. Nancy got one bra that was so old it crunched in her hands. We both laughed about this and made a deal to just take away Mom's crappy stuff because when she was gone we'd still have to deal with it. It made me feel better that at the very least I was not alone in getting broken or strange stuff from Mom.

Mom was also a collector of jackets. {I didn't think I would be lying if I said she has two hundred of them in her basement right now.} I know this because I saw downstairs in her basement and I asked, "Mom why do you have all of these? And this jacket?" It was very bright and colourful, but it was clearly a young child's jacket. Her answer? "Because I like the colours!" Mom laughed, a strange little flippant laugh and off she went, turning off the basement light, meaning it was time for me to leave. It was her secret place. No one was going downstairs unless she was right beside you. Nancy said Mom would give her Dad's old shoes, but they were not a pair, only one. We laughed, each mad a sad laugh, and decided it was time for a drink.

My sister and I were subjected to prolonged periods of unpredictable torment. How did it go so unseen by others? Mom could stop by, and we could have this wonderful time together, and yet I was left feeling like a zombie inside. These invisible feelings I carried knowing, that the odds always seem against me, and yet I didn't know why but I had such a strange devotion to my parents.

Humour and positive thoughts had helped me through some of my troublesome situations. Another great hiding spot, behind humour. I always tried to be funny. It has helped me through my pain. I married Phil and stayed for the long haul, and my parents pretty much stayed away.

* * *

Life was much better for me, and the years really went on. Dad was a proud strict and very controlling man. Mom played this lost, ditzy, confused woman to the outside world, but clever was what she was—very clever. She hid behind her kindness, and through her kindness she could inflict great pain. I would punish myself for thinking this way because Mom would do something nice and I would be lost again. I just didn't understand what was happening to me, so distance was the answer. I remember thinking that I would be okay and I guess I was for a time. I kept my distance.

CHAPTER 41:
I HAVE QUESTIONS

I met up with Nancy and I had questions. I was 50 years old and had this bad memory about my childhood and it was disturbing me and my sleep, which was again disturbed with nightmares. So very many nightmares.

We sat on my patio with a drink in hand. It was a beautiful day, but I was less than pleased. "Do you remember my nickname growing up?" I looked right into Nancy's eyes. I wanted the truth. Nancy looked at me, not even shocked that I would ask. She calmly said, "Do you remember mine?"

My eyes widened. I stared at her, feeling lost. This was unbelievable because I had no memory of Nancy having a nickname. I was thinking, *what was she saying? What does this mean?* So I asked, "Did you have a nickname too!" Nancy looked at me as if I should remember. "I don't remember your nickname." I was feeling stunned.

Once Nancy said her nickname, everything came flooding back. "Meathead, nothing but meat in my head." She looked at me for recollection.

"Oh, yes." I said. "Mine was stupid! That's right. Yours was meathead." I remembered her nickname, why had I forgotten this? We both laughed sadly.

EMILY KNEW

* * *

All the stories of my childhood that you have just read have come back to me in full force one way or another as I got older, and not in any order. This was the hard part for me, was putting thing in order for you to understand as best you can. At the same time, I am trying to give myself order so I can understand. This was incredibly difficult to do.

One bad memory after another, sometimes triggered by a smell or something that someone said or even by the way someone walked. Each memory came with weeks and sometimes months of me feeling a strange disorientation. My world would drift in and out of control. My stomach held most of this hurt, and I felt a tremendous amount of guilt or shame or something of that nature.

* * *

By the end of the day talking with Nancy, we both agreed that there was some form of neglect done by our parents. This was a really a hard thing to say out loud, and I did not understand why this was but what I have been telling you here is the truth. The peculiar thing for me was I felt Dad was the good guy because he had to stop Mom from getting after me more than once. Nancy said it was Dad who was the bad guy. I listened to what she had to say. it turned out that they were both bad at parenting. They were still our parents and children didn't come with any instructions. Plus, no one was perfect. My sister and I talked like we had never talked before and once again Nancy added that Evan didn't have it easy either. For some reason, it was hard for her to say. A certain part of us knew that being a parent could be hard to do sometimes, but still something sat uncomfortably on my mind.

I had continued to have what I learned were called flashbacks. A very persistent emotion had held me for a long time and it was frustrating. I was confronted with a mystery that wanted my attention.

I was alone again and trying to stay ahead of the games in life. After many years, my third marriage fell apart, and I was divorcing again my two children are grown up with children of their own. I had time to sit down and really think.

A strange event occurred that has awakened my memory more or less. I'd known about some of these things through these disturbing little movie clips of my childhood. I'd tried really hard to forget it all, moving as fast as I could without thinking about anything. *Let it go*, I thought, but it worried me. It worried me in ways that I had no words for. It was all inside of me. I'd hesitated in acting or saying something for way too long, maybe out of fear, maybe because I had caused so much trouble for my family as a child.

It was time for me to open up, even if doing so made me vulnerable. Distress had grabbed hold and the only relief from the affliction that I had secretly held was to talk with someone. I tried counsellors in schools and out of school, but I could find no voice.

One time with a counsellor, I had to sign a paper saying if they think you might hurt yourself they could lock you up. It was certainly not worded this way, but that was how I understood it. My thoughts on this were, *Get lost. Like I need someone else controlling me.* Which was totally unfair as I did feel that she really did want to help me. I truly wasn't strong enough to come forward at this time.

Friends I was luckier with; they have shown me a kindness like I'd never felt before. Two lady friends had me in the back seat of a car, pouring my heart out. I guess this was the kick-off for me to start to talk. I'd not really had many friends growing up. I'd always tried to keep my friends at a distance as I was aware that I was not like everyone else. I always felt like I was a heavy burden to have as a friend.

CHAPTER 42: FLASH WAY BACK!

I was a little girl and a girlfriend who had just moved in with her family that summer asked me if I would like to go with them to a movie. They were paying for me and everything and also lived just up the street, so I even had a ride home. I would just have to make sure that it was okay with my parents.

Oh wow. I was so excited to be part of something. I ran home to see if it was okay. It was a musical, this movie. I had no idea what that meant. My parents quickly pointed this out that there would be a lot of singing and said that I could not go. My heart sank and I started to cry. Dad said, "What are you crying for? You won't like this movie. It's all singing." He was not happy with me, but I stood there, crying with my head down. Now both of my parents are saying no. Dad said hotly, "Well, all right, you can go, but you won't like it with all that singing." By the way, neither Dad nor Mom sent me with any money to pay for any of it.

This movie was *The Sound of Music*. There was lots of singing and I loved it! Now, as I was writing this, I had another memory of going to see the movie *Bambi*.

I didn't get to see this movie as my parents and my-self plus one of my girlfriends were sitting in the theatre, feeling awful. Dad was getting mad. The movie didn't start at the time it was supposed to.

It was late, so he'd had enough. We up and left, drove back home in silence, never seeing this movie. If memory serves me right, I think this may have been on my birthday. This girlfriend never came near me again. My dad had scared her.

CHAPTER 43: NANCY'S MEMORIES

It's been very difficult having friends as we just didn't live on the same planet. Other kids could talk with their dad and mom, from what I noticed. None of us three kids were able to talk with our parents about anything, so we felt alone a lot. Other kids had parents who would come pick them up rather than walking. They would want to hear of the goings-on in their kids' days. I found myself reflecting on some of the things that Nancy and I talked about years earlier. Funny how we both have these strange stories about our parents. Nothing huge, it would seem, but once added together, something menacing was starting to take form and it broke my heart. Nancy was still mad that neither Dad nor Mom ever came to watch her doing her track and field nor did she ever get a ride home.

Nancy said that she had found Mom in the back yard this one time with her feet up, sitting in the sun eating a big banana split. Everything was on this banana split. Three different ice creams, the strawberries, whipped cream. Everything! If she didn't say anything about this ice cream treat, Nancy could have one too! "Don't tell anyone, shhh." Nancy couldn't understand why the whole family couldn't have what Mom was having, and I didn't understand this either. We only got desserts if we ate all our dinner.

It was just a small very unimportant thing, but it adds to a long list of whys. Nancy, I thought, felt bad for holding out on both Evan and I over this ice cream treat, but I knew it wasn't her fault. If you scored an ice cream, then good for you Nancy! Today, my sister and I love each other and both have a lot of fun when we get together even with these memories from our past.

Mom had no driver's licence for many years, and she would stress about the drive to the corner store or the bank. I didn't really understand all this. She always made it out to be somehow our fault that we were making her drive somewhere even though she didn't have a driver's licence. The same with money. It was up to us kids to bail out Mom after she bought lots of beautiful things for herself. So what did this make her? Selfish? Mean spirited?

Puzzling, it was so puzzling and the only life we knew! Mom wouldn't push an elevator button and would stand outside of the door until someone else came along so they could push the buttons. This wasn't over the top either, was it? Mom did not take any pictures with the camera unless asked and then only if she had to. If someone said, "I'll do it," Mom had no problem letting them. I had never heard Mom sing or even hum to a song, ever! Music appeared to have no effect on her, but strangely she could do dance steps. There were all kinds of silly little stuff like this, but nothing big on its own.

I could never own a black purse. Oh, I tried, and it didn't matter what size or shape. Mom went through every black purse that I ever owned. I finally gave up and have not owned a black purse for over twenty years now. If I showed up at a gathering with a black purse and set it down with other black purses, before I knew it, Mom would be inside my purse, saying, as she pulled out one thing after another, "This isn't mine. Oh no this isn't mine!" She would have a strange smile and she'd look at me from the corner of her eye and would keep pulling things out of my purse until I took it away from her. Didn't matter if everyone else had a black purse, it was just mine she'd do this with. Everyone would laugh and laugh, I laughed the first time, but as the years have moved on, it's not funny. This kind of stuff Mom liked doing and it became a lot over the years.

These memories would be gone out of my head, then something would trigger a memory and off I'd go to some strange place, trying to remember. Mom would say, "How are we going to manage? What are we going to do?" I heard this one the most: "What are we going to do? Oh, what are we going to do?" It would be about money, always about money. Nancy heard more on having babies—"Don't hurt her for having babies." Me too, but not as much as Nancy.

When he was a little kid, Evan had one of Mom's high heel shoes and started hitting Nancy on top of her head with the heel of said shoe. Nancy said she cried out for help, but he would hit her harder each time. Finally, Mom came into the room. Nancy got a spanking and sent to bed. What? Why her and not Evan? Nancy found this to be very confusing to look back on and told me so.

Life was hard, darn hard, and always so confusing. How can this be put into words? It's like we were playing some sort of game without knowing any of the rules and those rules could change at any time. This had not been a happy or fun game to play. Mom let our brother have anything and everything, it would seem. I was told by Nancy that Evan sure didn't have it easy either and the way she said this to me was like it was too dark to tell. Nancy knew things, but it was hard to talk about it. I could see the worried look come to her eyebrows. Nancy would get really upset about this unfair treatment, and her questions were many when she was a child and still even as an adult. She really was trying hard to understand what was happening in our house. I feel bad now because I didn't stand by her and she was right to question things. I guess I was too scared. It would seem to me that sometimes you had to save yourself. This doesn't mean you didn't feel for each other, but sadly you were glad it wasn't you that time.

Nancy did finally find out the date of her birth. It was when she turned sixteen and was going for her driver's licence. That's when Mom had to hand over her birth certificate. Nancy was sixteen! Why had Mom played this game with her? It was so very mean! The years of her crying over this, begging Mom to tell her what day she was born. Like my nightmares. So many years of this. The Christmas gift with the white fuzzy stuff was Kotex. Who gives Kotex as a Christmas gift? Mom did, but why was it funny to see your little girls crying on Christmas morning? Mom never said sorry for this either.

Dad would fight a lot with Evan; it seemed mostly over tools, as I recall. These were terrible fights. I didn't stay around for those. It was like I would shrink. For some reason, I couldn't explain the control and manipulation our parents had over us. Mom seemed to be able to affect me with the tone in her voice or just a look. Yet, strangely, I felt I had to stay close, like they were the only people in the world who knew that there was something wrong with me.

How could I have friends when my world didn't match theirs? They didn't feel the same way I did about family. This made me wonder all the more about what was wrong with me. I had speech difficulties and memory glitches. Still do. I felt my parents understood me and would have my best interests at heart. Don't get me wrong. We did have some good times. Dad had a few sayings, like this one on New Year's Eve night. He would tell me if I did the dishes tonight he would do them for the rest of the year, which was not fair. I didn't know what New Year's is. Another was first one to bed and falls asleep gets the candy, and it was Dad every time who got the candy. In the morning he said he was the first one asleep. I would laugh as I knew it was funny. Or there were these ones: go out and play in traffic, or take a long walk on a short pier. I always took these with great fun because you had to figure them out.

* * *

I was not sure how old I was, but I stood on a chair not only for dishes but the stove. I sometimes sat on the counter beside the stove so I could sit and stir whatever I was cooking, it was a little scary as the stove got hot. Well, for goodness sake, how old was I? Every flashback came with so many questions. All of them seemed to be unanswered, and I would feel the ground go out from under me because something was dreadfully wrong. This was another thing I learned later. Nancy said, "You were always kept in your room. I don't remember seeing much of you as a baby."

Oh good. I didn't know that I was kept in my bedroom. Was this why I almost failed kindergarten? Was this why I was so excited to talk with other little kids? Was this why I didn't fit in at my first birthday party? And was this why I just sat in her bedroom because it was the only room I felt safe in? My head hurt. I found myself feeling like I should curl up into a ball and stay sad forever with so many questions.

I could never stay the night at a friend's house. Just the thought of staying at someone else's house made me feel really sick and I'd want to cry. Nancy tells me she started off having this trouble too, but then as it turned out she would rather be at anyone's house but ours. I kept thinking that when I would get home the next day everyone would be gone and the house would be empty. I worried about being left behind, then there would no one in my life. I also didn't know what kind of monsters lived at other people's houses and I was having enough troubles with the monsters that wandered around ours. I didn't know all the hiding spots. Let me tell you, I worked hard finding just the right hiding spots. The thought of staying away from home terrorized me. Sleep would not come when I did try, and the night would drag on. I didn't sleep like the other kids, either. I just couldn't make myself sleep. I wasn't brave enough and I'd long since given up sleeping through the night. Even now that I am an adult, I do most of my writing in the dark of the midnight hour. To be quite honest, I get up late at night sometimes and wander about in the summer months. I like the feel of the grass on my feet. It's so peaceful and the stars at night are beautiful. The only thing that could make this better would be the sound of a little creek. I would feel almost childlike, arms high up in the air, breathing deeply, free ... and I was an adult, with the start of greying hair, but the heart of a child.

I never did find out what Social Services was as a child. My mom told me that the neighbours said they would call Social Services and I'd be taken away. Maybe that's why I was looking for so many hiding spots for all those years. Like so many other things in my life, I had no idea, and no one was going to tell me, and I was too afraid to ask. The Joneses, our neighbours, moved away the following year in the spring. They apparently couldn't handle looking across the street and seeing all the things that went on at our house at night. I couldn't understand why they felt that way.

These nightmares of walls crushing down on rubber, really tightly squeezed rubber, I could hear this. All those years, all those nights, I would be soaked in sweat, horrified and afraid to fall asleep. Why was I having these awful nightmares? Something unknown was still inside of me. I told Nancy about when I was first came home with my newborn baby, Jenny. I told her about Mom telling me that I should expect Jenny to be dead in the morning. This was another one of those flashbacks.

Nancy's voice cracked with strain. She looked sad, and her eyebrows pulled together. She said, "I didn't know that Mom was doing that to you too!"

We didn't say much, only a little after that, because there it was that strange silence that we both carry. My radar was up and I felt I must go for the truth. I didn't want to hurt my sister by asking too many uncomfortable questions. We changed the subject and I was left wondering if maybe Mom lost a baby or was it just that our parents didn't respect proper boundaries?

CHAPTER 44: OUR CHERRY TREE GRANDPARENTS

The grandparents with the big cherry tree were my dad's parents. Grandpa had a beautiful garden and a fantastic large yard, plus a big cherry tree. Grandpa would walk me around his garden, telling me the names of flowers, and showing me what our vegetables looked like as plants. We kids were told to behave by Dad, and we did, staying outside until told otherwise. On sunny days, they played grass bowling. I was too little for this game. It was so nice sitting in the beautiful gardens watching. This was always a wonderful time, and I'd get excited about visiting with them. We kids were given some money and could walk down for ice cream at the corner store.

Grandma, on the other hand, I didn't think she ever left her kitchen much. Grandma was a really good cook; her home always smelled so good. I was afraid to say anything because I sure didn't want to disappoint them. I liked visiting with them even if we did have to be really quiet. Grandma made the best chocolate cake ever. Anything she cooked was great!

I remember Grandma and Grandpa with the big cherry tree with many good thoughts. I was allowed to play card games, and they let me be part of the family. These very same grandparents went to this place called a church. My parents made it sound awful, full of people taking money from the gullible and always having their hands in people's wallets. We went to grandma's and Grandpa's church it was a party for their anniversary. These church people were giving our grandparents a party. I was not sure which year, but a big one and it was fun, especially all the people I got to meet. Grandma introduced me around to all her friends. They had said nice things to me. I found this all very confusing. I wondered why my dad and mom hated the church so much and why I didn't feel the same about this. This would be another thing I would not dare ask my parents because I'd heard them talking of this church stuff. It sounded pretty scary, like they were very sneaky people. I knew asking questions like Nancy did only got you hurt answers but, as always, I wondered why .

CHAPTER 45: BALLOONS! WHY?

My mind raced off to balloons. Why was I thinking about balloons? These flashbacks were running me over, but now I was listening and trying very hard to understand what it all meant. I didn't remember any of us having a birthday party. Now this didn't mean we didn't have any, just because I just didn't remember things. Or was it something else? Balloons. Nothing more. Just thinking about balloons. My feelings and memories were puzzling, to say the very least! I didn't have a clue why I was sitting here wondering about balloons but I was.

Okay I did remember one sleep-over birthday party that I had, and Evan helped me put it on. I was not sure what age I was—a teenager was my best guess. Dad and Mom were not home, so Evan came downstairs to see how things were going with my birthday party. I had a few friends who came to stay the night and couldn't have been more delighted. I had no idea how to have a party, but at this time in my life I guess I was willing enough to give it a try.

To my great surprise, Evan turned off the lights and told us scary stories walking back and forth with a flashlight tucked under his chin. I was happy he cared enough to do this for me and my party. We were in our sleeping bags on the floor, quietly listening as he walked back and forth. The ending of his stories ended with - boo or something that made us all jump. I thought it was super fantastic, but my friends were really scared. I couldn't understand what they were afraid of. I knew what scary was and this wasn't even close. I didn't think I had any other sleepovers after that. If I did, I sure didn't remember.

Why was I sitting here thinking about balloons?

Evan had a rage when you tried to wake him up in the mornings. He would throw things—a glass or a lamp—crash at whoever was in the room waking him! I never worried about waking Evan because I was so fast on my feet and could duck.

There were a few days Evan really struggled. Something was eating at him. I overheard him talking to Mom in our backyard. Evan was very upset, so much so that he thought he needed to see a psychiatrist. He was almost crying. I didn't understand the things that were happening in his life when he was young and didn't hear enough about what was bothering him. Mom was standing with that strange look of almost pleased, just like when Nancy would cry about Mom didn't remember the day she was born. Nancy said Evan did not have things easy. I was puzzling over this too, because that's all she would say. I understood but I didn't understand. Life was just so darn hard. Nancy said that Dad was tough on him. "Little boy never cry, or I'll give you a reason to cry." I do remember hearing that, and that little girls should be seen not heard! Evan and Dad did a lot of that play fighting. I never liked it when they did this. I wondered if Evan liked it. I found this to be a stressful situation, but somehow I would be locked in and watching.

Evan was also my tooth fairy when I was young. It was great fun. The door would fly open, and he would stomp into my bedroom, flapping his arms like wings, and grab my pillow out from under my head. He'd put some money down and stomp out, still flapping his wings, through the pillow back at me, and I would laugh.

Nancy and I, when we had babies of our own, we had laughed about this, with Barry teasing both Nancy and I about men and their needs. We thought of Mom as being crazy or goofy or just plain old silly. They were our dad and mom and all that we have learned we have learned from them. Mom always said things that were a little bit mean, but we didn't think any of this was on purpose; because of her childhood, she had troubles. We did think there was something not quite right about Mom, but we loved her anyway. She was our Mom. Dad was harder to get close to. He always kept his distance from us kids. Dad was funny in a sarcastic way, with a dry sense of humour. I do remember Dad saying to Mom that he didn't know what was going on with us kids. He told Mom, "You always keep them away from me." Maybe that's why I followed him around so much when I was younger. I think that I liked the fact that Dad could laugh out loud and Mom never could.

Dinners with our parents as grandparents was way different. WAY and UNBELIEVABLY different. Dad would clown around with the grandkids at the table. The difference between Christmas dinners with Dad's parents, with polite chatter, and the dead silence from when we were little kids—there was no comparison. It was a creepy, stressful fun. Well, who knew Dad could have fun at a dinner table? I did say this and more than once, "These are not the same people that raised us!" Not even close. Things did change once we were all out of the house and sometimes I would think that I'd got things all wrong and push back all those silly memories. I had good memories here, but what was with these awful nightmares. Why was I still having them?

Evan and Nancy and their spouses helped me a lot when we had children of our own because I was in for years of struggles. But, strangely, my parents would help me when things went bad. I was still the troubled person, and my family knew it. I would make jokes about Mom and how she liked to have a front-row seat to anything that blew up in my face. I would then feel mean about saying this because Mom could be so very nice. I have a hard time with this. *Why does Mom sometimes care and then she kicks the rug right out from under me? Why?* Yes there were many, many times I wondered why? It's hard trying to understand all the whys. I was not suicidal, but I would be lying if I didn't say life could sure take you down sometimes. I would have to pick myself up and start all over again, put a smile back on my face and get on with it, even if I at the same time felt frozen.

CHAPTER 46: THE QUESTIONS PILE UP

Nancy and I had talked about trying to hide money away from Mom, but she was good at finding it tucked behind a picture hanging on the wall or stuffed into a stuffed toy. We were looking at our own children and they were heading off to the camp store for ice cream. Handing them some money, we couldn't help but think about how it was when we were little. It was like these memories jumped out of nowhere and took hold. It was like Mom could smell where the money was hiding. I told my sister that I had hidden money in a rolled up sock, but Mom found it and it was gone.

It's awful when you have money troubles in a house, but deep down we knew that something else was at play. Try as we might, understanding things always seemed out of reach. Then Mom would do something nice like say, "If you girls want to go to town, I'll watch the kids" because the men were fishing. Then we would feel bad about saying not nice things about Mom; the guilt was awful.

It seemed to me that if I got stuck thinking about these strange things too much, I not only had nightmares but severe headaches. I later learned these headaches were called migraines. I didn't know what was happening to me but let me tell you they were very painful. I had no answers for all the whys in my life. I'd been tormented by these thoughts of strangeness my whole life. Evan was the firstborn and he came early and almost died. Could this be why Mom had said what she had about our babies dying? But why scare the daylights out of us? I did not understand and did I not tell my sister or anybody what Mom had said for a good many years. Why did I not tell anyone? It wasn't until our children had grown up and were out of the house that Nancy and I could talk. Why couldn't we talk about these things for all these years? This really puzzled me and I hurt trying to understand. Maybe it was just too much to handle that it took so much time to figure out.

It seemed for a while that whenever Nancy and I got together there was some new memory from one of us and we did talk a little. It was bits and pieces and some seemed so unimportant, but were they? These traps set for us seemed to come right out of the blue, and sometimes they would jump out of nowhere and knock me right off my feet. This was disturbing and confusing to say the very least, and would trigger strange feeling deep inside of me. Oh so very lost!

I wished they would go away, these strange memories, and the nightmares too! I was confused, but I was fighting harder now to understand, I know our life as children was not great but we made it. I really had no parents at all growing up, and I understood that now. Evan and Nancy also had no parents to speak of. I also know life isn't perfect and we all make mistakes. I was trying to do what everyone says to do: "Let it go! Find some balance in your life." I very much wanted balance in my life, and I really wanted to let it all go. This sounded so easy and wonderful and nice. Just let it all go! But question kept piling up. Why?

CHAPTER 47: GAMES OTHERS PLAY WITH OUR HEARTS

My third marriage was full of work lots and lots of hard work, but I could really breathe. I was far enough away from my parents that a phone call would be needed and they couldn't be just dropping in. I was getting to know some new people and felt maybe life would be okay. I'd started writing letters to Mom and some friends too! I wrote everyone I had an address to. Okay, it was a dying art with these new computers and email and all this interesting stuff. They said email was the new way to go, but when you share a computer with a not-so-sharing person, you write letters. Well, one-way letter-writing mostly; I didn't get many letters back. Like I said, it's a dying art.

It was the best way to stay in touch with my mother, however. She couldn't say anything to mess with my head. I think that I was finding that balance that everyone talks about. I can maybe let it go forgive and move into a happier life. Once in a while I would talk on the phone with Mom, but only once in a long while. It was working out much better, well almost, you know. I still got these nightmares from time to time but I'd learned how to stop them—kind of change the channel or I could wake myself up. Then I'd just stay awake for a few hours before going back to sleep. Yup, I thought maybe I would make it after all.

I phoned Mom to say that we were coming over for a visit. This would be in the springtime, and we would also go visit with his family too. I would phone Mom again just to let her know this weekend and on Saturday. So Mom *knew* Saturday and which Saturday we would be there! I felt I had covered all my basics and that Mom knew just what I was saying. I truly was working on this "let it go" thing.

Mom would cook a dinner and invite Evan and his wife plus a friend or two. They would wait, and I was told that Mom would be saying things like, "Well, I wonder where Emily is?" She would hold up dinner and appear to be stressing about where are we. They would sit down to this meal on Friday. Yes, Friday! No matter how hard I tried to tell her Saturday, she would always cook dinner the night before I was to arrive. Why would she do this? Oh sure, this was funny. It's only such a small thing, but it was as funny as my black purse for me.

I would get there on Saturday. This was not so funny for other people. Some people were mad at me because I didn't show up for dinner and because I had worried my mom. I would say, "But I told her I was coming on Saturday." They would say, "You know your mother gets lost sometimes. You should have called her anyway." I could never win; it became very stressful again for me. I hurt in ways others couldn't understand.

This happened over and over again. This was not funny for me at all and I would feel frustrated, not knowing what I could do. Why Mom would cook dinner and invite people for Friday? I might never understand this. What was the use in calling? Even if I made Mom repeat Saturday to me, she would still cook dinner the night before. This was her game, the game I'd been playing my whole life. The rules change and only Mom knew the rules. I guess I kept showing up or kept my parents in my life because I just had to understand and I so desperately need answers. I wanted answers, so I stubbornly hung in there.

I thought I could beat her at her own game by just showing up. No phone calls. It'd be a surprise. I would tell Evan, heck, beg him not to say anything to Mom. So I had stopped calling before our trips to visit, and this worked out much better. I didn't have anyone giving me heartache about Mom's dinners. I felt back on my feet again, but this only lasted a few visits.

So Mom switched things up, she then would phone saying that Nancy and Barry would be coming up for a visit right around the time that we would be making the trip. I very much wanted to see Nancy and Barry when they came up from the city for a visit. It would be all of us together—my brother and his wife and my sister and her husband. I was on my husband right away for an unplanned trip. Oh, he was not happy, but we would go because I so wanted to get together with both Evan and Nancy. I had a burning desire to do this.

So with much trouble, we would drive over and get there with plenty of time for a good visit before returning home. I was excited, thinking how much fun it would be getting together as I didn't have many friends who understood me like my family did. Once there and settling in, I wondered where Barry was and no Nancy. I asked Mom, "When do Barry and Nancy arrive?" Clearly I was thrilled we would all be together because Nancy was the closest to a friend I had and I had not seen her in some time. "Oh," Mom said. "Nancy had a doctor's appointment and they couldn't make it." If Evan knew that Nancy and Barry were coming, he never let on nor did we talk about this because, after all, these things can happen.

I was disappointed, but these things happened, and happened and happened and happened! Just like the Friday dinner parties, Mom found a new way. She had managed to fool me with her new game. I think it happened about four times and then I lost it. I thought Nancy was blowing me off or she does not want to visit with me. My husband was not happy because of me as well. That was it! Once back home, I phoned Nancy and said, "What is it with you? Where were you this weekend? Is it because you just don't want to see me? We keep driving over and you keep backing out. Why, Nancy?"

Nancy said, "What are you talking about?"

I was still mad at her and wanted answers. "Every time Mom said you and Barry would be making the trip up, we also drove over because I wanted to see you, but you keep cancelling. WHY?"

I was not happy with Nancy and I was blasting her and she had no idea what I was talking about. Nancy then said, "Emily, we have not been invited up for years."

"What? But Mom said…" I told her. "She called me to say that you were coming up for a visit. And every time I race over to see you and Barry only to hear you can't make it because of this or that or doctor appointments. Why would she do this?"

WHY? I was no longer mad at Nancy. My voice dropped low and here came this sick feeling, creeping over me. *Oh Nancy, I am so sorry.* I sat down. "Nancy, I'm sorry I got mad at you. Why would Mom do this?"

Nancy had no idea either. I hung up the phone and just sat there, completely lost. My husband at this time was mad at me for making him take these unplanned trips to disappointments. I unjustly got mad at Nancy and she had no idea what'd been going on. Why was Mom doing these things and why was it I didn't see it coming?

I had been writing Mom letters and I tried with all my heart to say nothing in them. I only phoned if I thought I absolutely had to. The distance was growing but I was still sinking deeper into a depressed state, and I was well aware that I was not letting it all go like everyone seemed to think I should be doing. In some ways, it was a relief not keeping in touch, but in other ways I was so lost and I hurt because I just didn't understand what was happening.

I wanted family and it seemed that everyone else had family. I felt a relief not phoning Mom or staying in touch, but this was very short lived. I wanted very much to have this family thing and there were times when Dad and Mom were almost real people with feelings but always with some sort of trap. Mother's and Father's Day cards are another thing that I find impossible to buy. Year after year I would stand in front of these beautiful cards and wonder why this was so hard for me to do. I would read them, but none seemed to say how I was feeling. Why was this so hard?

CHAPTER 48: WHAT WOULD NORMAL PEOPLE DO?

We had headed over to visit Dad and Mom and Evan's place as they both lived on the same property; that's where their business was. I went without calling ahead of time for our usual visit and to my surprise, they were not living in their house anymore but someone else was, so we ended up at Evan's place. Dad and Mom were gone.

"Dad and Mom don't live here anymore. They moved," Evan told us. What? They had moved without saying one word about moving! Not one word! Who does this? They moved, where did they move to? Evan told us where they were now living, which was only a few miles away. I had no feelings. Just frozen. Evan didn't give any reason for this move.

I was suspicious because we three had been raised to not trust each other. Mom had told me that Evan has a bad temper and Nancy was selfish, but I was starting to think she was the smart one because she kept her distance from all of us. Evan had long since got hold of his temper and I suppose both my brother and sister were told things about me too. They would have been told that I was stupid or of this nature; all of these things would ring true. We were given half-truths so it was easier to believe the lies. Dad died before I got him all figured out, but he must have enjoyed our discomfort or Mom's lies. Even though we three children tried to be close, we had a built in mistrust for each other.

To me, their moving without saying anything was a craziness I just couldn't understand. It was just plain spiteful. I had to fight my husband to do these visits and then my parents did something like this. It was stinging right into my heart. Why would they do this? You can't imagine the despair I felt at these sick games my parents liked to play.

We drove to their new home and it got even stranger. I asked, "Why didn't you say you were moving?" I was not happy about this.

Mom said, "Oh, we knew you were busy." Then the subject was changed quickly and Mom walked away into the kitchen, leaving me standing there.

I sat down at the table and I was totally stunned, perplexed … so taken aback. Again, there really aren't enough words. Dad was at the table. We sat down. I was numb. Thinking back now, we were not shown around their new place, either. Don't most "normal" people show you around, saying things like "It's has a nice big bathroom or look out this window at the view or I'm still unpacking but want to change this room into?" Anyone one of these are generally heard from newly moved in normal people. Right? I couldn't help but think they couldn't even move like normal people. We drove away after having had a quick cup of coffee. It was a very uncomfortable cup of coffee and now my husband was not talking. He didn't care how I was feeling and he thought I was dumb for wanting to see them anyway.

I felt quite empty and didn't know if I had any feelings left anymore, yet the stress was somehow building in me. Why would my dad and mom want me to feel this way? How long have they lived here? They'd had a yard sale, I heard, and it was quite a move. I knew deep in my heart that things were not right and now it was like I was looking for something that I could say that would make someone believe me. I did try and I did talk about some of these strange things, but for some reason it just made me look bad in their eyes. Let's face it. Mom going through my purse was funny and everyone laughed and so did I the first time. Mom screwing up dinner, well maybe she was just busy and forgot. That they moved and didn't ask for our help was wonderful in some people's eyes because they thought we were so busy. My parents were well liked and lots of people thanked them for the things they did for them. People thought my parents were the best because of their kindness in going into schools to teach dance with the kids or doing the same thing at an old folk home. They would go out of their way to help other people. It was so confusing to live with them and hear time and time again what great parents they were and how helpful they have been. I could cry just thinking about this because I didn't feel this way. Why?

Then, only a few years later, they did it again. They had moved again without saying a single word. We went to their house and someone else was living there. This time I was so hurt all I could do was laugh sadly and hate them.

I did feel better when I spoke about this with Nancy, about my hurt—or was it shame—from being left out, Was I so unimportant to them? I was struggling to handle all the hurt feelings piling up in me. Was it that my parents just hated me? I phoned Nancy, her and I both had no idea they had moved *twice* without telling us. Nancy was just as shocked and as hurt as I was. There it was, wasn't it? We were never their girls; they didn't like girls. Little girls should be seen and not heard. That's what Dad said all the time. Nancy and I never were part of this family. Simply little toys to damage emotionally.

This second move, I had so many mixed feelings and my world was spinning apart in the confusion. I just didn't care anymore. Even saying this was a lie and I knew it. It was a kind of hurt that made you want to throw your hands in the air and walk away forever. It hurt and I didn't understand and I didn't walk away, and for the life of me I didn't know why. I was drawn into this craziness, I think it's because I wanted answers. Even if it hurt, I wanted answers. I had a real need for answers! *Please, somebody help me?* Once again, I'd tried to talk about these strange things with my parents but no matter what I tried to say, it always come out that I should just let it go and get on with my life. I so wanted to be part of a family and to feel the way my friends felt for their parents.

* * *

"Evan won't look at his baby pictures." Mom had said this many times, just another one of those things she liked to just throw into the air. Evan did not have children of his own and my guess was he didn't want to pass on a life of confusion and stress to his child. So I felt no reason to ask questions when I felt I knew the answer, but somehow I knew it was of importance. There were many days that I was left wondering why, and I couldn't let it go. I was wishing hadn't brought children onto this awful planet and hoping I didn't hurt them as much as I was hurt. I loved my children very much and wanted the very best for them. I was aware that I was not smart, and even as an adult I struggled with my bad memory. New words still caused my tongue troubles. I wanted to be close to my kids but felt the less they were around me the better for then. I hoped that I didn't live too long and then I'd know that my kids would be free of me as I wanted to be free of mine.

I didn't know if this was important or not, but both Evan and I were not afraid of dying. Evan spoke up at dinner one evening. Out of the blue, he said, "I'm not afraid of dying."

I responded right after him. "Me either." I so understand what Evan said. "When you live the way we have, with no ground to stand on, life is not worth it. No one can understand and it feels like there is no hope of ever getting away." I was trapped in a circle of my parents doing something to help and almost nice, to having everything blow up in your face and it looking like you caused it all.

I didn't know how Nancy felt about death. I had a hard time with funerals, because most times I wondered if they weren't the lucky ones. I have had good times, but life has been so strange, hard. This same dinner, Evan said to Mom, "Someone drove into your driveway fence post." Mom had a new chain link fence put around her place, right up to her driveway, with a gate. Something had happened to her driveway post. She responded quickly about this damage. "It was the garbage man."

Evan smiled and added, "The hit came from inside of your yard."

Mom glanced over to me sharply, then paused briefly and answered fast, "It was Barry."

I laughed out loud because Barry and I had at times driven Mom's car for her, but Barry was not here to say anything. I quickly responded, "Oh, I saw that. You blamed Barry because he's not here." Everyone laughed and I didn't know where to look. I think maybe I was excited because Evan had caught her in a lie. We all know that Mom was the one who had driven into the fence post but there was no way Mom ever going to say it was her. Even when she knew she been caught, Mom looked innocent and stuck to her lie. It was always the same. Mom blamed others even when it was apparent it was her fault.

I wondered why my brother had brought this up, but I was somehow tickled that he did. Once again, everyone at the table laughed because it was just not that big a deal.

* * *

Evan when Evan was a teenager, I had good memories of riding in his car. Evan even took me to the A&W a few times. If it wasn't for him, I would never have had an A&W experience as a kid or got out of the house, for that matter. Evan had a job at Brown's Chicken, if I recall the name right. It was great. I liked the taste of this and sometimes he would bring some home food after work. It was wonderful to eat. Yup, Evan was indeed good in our family. That was how I saw it as a child. He carried the load that our parents never did. Nancy and Barry were good to me as well; we formed our own kind of fun and understanding of each other as we grew older.

Oh one thing that my brother had talked about over the years was that he had trouble with his right eye. He said that it has a black round hole in the middle with white floating things blocking his view. For some reason I didn't understand, I never asked him about his eye, maybe because Mom said, "Evan must have inherited Dad's bad eye."

I remembered Dad going to a doctor because he lost sight in one of his eyes when we were kids at home. Dad talked about how the doctor took his eye out and it sat on his cheek. This news really creeped me out, so I believed it to be true. Like I always did, I asked nothing about why Evan's eye was like that.

CHAPTER 49:
LOVE ME, LOVE ME NOT

My third husband and myself had driven the four hours over for a short visit with my parents, a cup of coffee, then were on our way to visit and stay with his parents for a while. The anxiety to plan these trips would cause me so much upset that I would have diarrhoea for days! I'd be sick with worry as I just didn't know how my parents would behave and my husband was mad at me for wanting to go in the first place. Never to disappoint, that's for sure. My anxiety just kept growing and my parents could hardly wait to give me a good kick in the face.

It was a beautiful sunny day when we arrived and Evan was visiting too. They were sitting at the kitchen table and the sliding glass door was wide open. We could hear laughter as we were coming up the steps. I was smiling and could feel myself relax a little. They knew we were coming today and they sound happy. What could go wrong? It's a quick cup of coffee! I got just outside their sliding door and looked inside with a feeling of relief as everyone was in a good mood. *Thank you, God. Thank you, God.* Saying hi, I walked inside, my husband right behind me.

The first words out of my dad's mouth were, "Here she is, our spare body parts!"

Everyone was laughing. I stopped dead in my tracks and it must have shown on my face as the subject got changed quickly. Everyone was laughing, including my husband. The feelings that I had I didn't have words for. Was it disbelief? Sadly, it was true, though, wasn't it? I was seen as spare body parts. This was all I was to my parents; the way they see me. And my husband thought this funny as well. I had to fight my husband to get over to visit with them only so they could prove that he was right.

Why would I want anything to do with them? Why did I keep coming back? Would they actually ask me if they needed body parts? Would this give them joy, cutting my flesh open and take pieces out of me? This was one of my really saddest heartbreaking trips. Even my husband thought nothing about me being someone's spare body parts. Or maybe he was happy because he was right, I was fighting for approval or acceptance. I guess that's what I was trying for, what I'd spent a lifetime trying to do. Dare I say, get love from my parents?

* * *

They did come and visit us at our camping business with their fifth wheel. I was happy for them as they got their chance to travel. Okay that was what silly me was thinking. They stopped by to visit. I was thinking that they should be happy for me too. Dad and Mom were with their friends and were parked out front having their lunch. I barely got to see them. My husband came to the office. Dad and Mom were having lunch, so I said I needed to get some change. I was gone five or ten minutes. When I got back, they were gone.

I walked up to my husband, saying, "Where did they go?"

He replied, "They said a quick goodbye me him and just up and left."

They didn't say anything about being in a hurry and didn't bother to say goodbye to me. I was lost again in this whirlwind. Why did they do this? Was it just to make sure I knew how unimportant I am.

My husband thought I was an idiot for even caring about them and let me know this. He walked away, shaking his head, and I sank. Yes, this hurt me more and puzzled me greatly. I was really getting tired of their strange behaviour. It was so darn draining. I was so hurt that at night when everyone else was sleeping I'd cry my eyes out and wake to the make-up stains on the pillowcase. Things were not getting any better.

CHAPTER 50: MAKING CHRISTMAS MEMORIES

Mom had called and it'd been a long time since we'd talked. Dad was sick and not doing well. The doctors said Dad had around two years to live. I was shocked, but not like you would think. My first thought, when hearing this news, was, *Will Dad die and never say sorry for the way I was raised!* I was surprised by my way of thinking, but that was the truth! It wasn't like I hadn't had years to figured out that my parent did and said some pretty strange things, but I wasn't aware that I was even thinking this way. I was confused by this thought and where it was coming from and now I felt guilty and ashamed of myself because Dad was dying. Forgiving was the right thing to do and I tried to let all these unimportant things go.

As my Christmas gift to both my parents after hearing this news, I started a photo album of all of us family and friends, grandchildren growing up. I wrote a poem for the photo album and some jokes. In short, I filled this photo album with love and good memories. I was trying with all my heart to find good memories. This would be my Christmas gift to both my parents this year. After all, Dad was dying and what was left now, I was thinking, was memories. I so desperately wanted to have some good ones. Mom called while I was just finishing up this photo album and I was cleaning up the pictures spread all over my kitchen table. I was feeling quite pleased with myself.

She was inviting us to come for Christmas at Evan's house. I was thrilled. We had not been invited to Christmas for years. I really wanted to be there when they opened my gift. I saw us talking about all the good memories with each picture that we looked at. So I said to Mom, "I'll check with my husband and get back to you. I think this will be great. I'll call you tomorrow."

I was clearly excited and really wanted to come over for Christmas this year, not because of my parents, but I wanted to see Evan. I still enjoyed being around him. I did talk with my husband and it was a bit of a deal, but in the end, if we had no snowstorms, then okay we would go. I was pretty happy about this. My photo gift was done. Time to wrap it up and pick up the pictures from the table. Not even an hour had passed and the phone rang. It was Mom. Puzzled, as I had said that I would call her back tomorrow, I excitedly said, "Sounds like we can make it as long as there is no snow storm." I was very happy and really looking forward to this.

"Oh, you are going come then." She paused. Something about her flat voice sent my mind on a questioning overdrive. "Well, don't mind that I give better gifts to Evan. It's because we get better gifts from him. As long as that's okay."

My heart sank, my eyebrows frowned. What? Why would anyone phone and say that? I felt as if a sinkhole had appeared beneath me and I was being sucked down into craziness, wracking my damaged memory for details that never came. I was sinking right into the floor. I was completely off-balance. It was a very disturbing feeling and I knew it well. I didn't cry, but I didn't say anything. I was confused and so very lost and I wondered if Evan even knew that we were invited.

Why did she do this? She must have known how much she was hurting me. Was this fun for her? Mom was a sick person and I was not going anywhere and I didn't understand how she could be like this? I didn't know if I hated her. I felt sorry for her as she was sick and I wondered what happened in her life to make her this way. I was trying to forgive and forget, but this was not working for me. I stubbornly hung in there because I needed answers. My despair kept on growing. Why was it that so many people loved my dad and mom? Why was it I couldn't feel the same way?

My husband was happy about not going and could not understand why I wanted to visit with them anyway. But, truth be told, my husband didn't do anything much at Christmas, so anything was better than nothing. I didn't tell my husband what my mom said. I hate to say this but he was right; I had rotten parents. Was my mom plan old evil? I packed up their gift and sent it by mail.

A year or so later, when Dad was in the hospital dying and I was now living with Mom. I was divorcing my husband. We'd had a big fight and he had said that he won't allow me to go and visit my dad. He used those words and it was like I woke up and knew he had never really loved me. I just looked good on his arm. I felt I had nowhere else to go. I had no money; everything in the bank was frozen. Who would take me in? Mom did and she was being quite helpful. I was completely lost. My life was spinning out of control and I was very grateful for my mom's help.

That's when, out of the blue, Mom said, "Oh yeah, that photo album that you gave us for Christmas—Dad and I did look at it. He thought it was nice."

I knew she was talking about my Christmas gift from a year ago. Why bring it up now? I must have looked happy or something. Was I smiling Mom? Did you feel a need to step on me? I used to try to please her different personalities, between nice and mean, so as to keep the peace. I felt nothing!

CHAPTER 51: STRANGE THINGS

It was my grown-up daughter who made me aware of how I got turned around. I had gone down to for a visit with her and had my two dogs with me. I was going through one heck of an ugly divorce from husband number three and living with my mother. So I said to my daughter, "I need to take the dogs for a walk," while she was busy finishing up her work for the day.

She handed me a map of the city blocks around her apartment and said, "Here Mom you'll need this!"

I thought about how funny she was. Why would I need this? I wouldn't be going that far but I took it and thanked her. Once outside and walking, I realized how right she was. I was turned around in no time at all and looking at this map, but it was more than that. I didn't know how many times I put the map into my pocket, but I kept bringing it out and looking at it. I was puzzled. This was the same feeling I had when my friends told me that I locked doors.

Why was it that I didn't know these things about myself but everyone else sees something? Oh God, here we go. What's wrong with me? The agony of knowing and not knowing—some days, I felt like I lived with ghosts! It baffled me quite a bit as to what was it that she knew about me that I was not aware of. How did Jenny know about me getting lost? I was stumped. There was that off-balance feeling again. I made it back to Jenny's. I was not like everyone else; I was different somehow. This made me want to sit right down and cry. My memory was hit and miss. I could look at something I'd seen many times, but for some reason that memory was gone. I stood staring, knowing that I should remember, but it's just not there. I had a feeling of recollection, but I couldn't pull it out of my brain and I still had this happen from time to time.

These strange things kept coming up in my life. I was unhinged. My mental discomfort. it was growing inside me. Subconsciously, I wanted answers and I needed a solution to these issues. It hadn't changed over the years, but I had noticed that if I was tired or upset, my memory was gone. I sometimes felt that I could go catatonic, into a new hiding space inside my head. It was getting hard to move with these confusing thoughts. I could go so deep within myself I feared I might never come back out.

I could drive my car and buy food at a store. I could even talk with other people, but I was dying inside. It was really scary and calming at the same time. I wished sometimes that all my feelings could go away. Then at least I would have some peace. How did one tell other people about knowing but not knowing at the same time? I turned three street corners. I was lost. Heck, even if I walked straight up three blocks. I felt uneasy. I always felt uneasy and I always got lost. There it was again, this same feeling that something was wrong with me. What was it with these nightmares? I wondered what had happened to me. The years kept rolling on.

* * *

Mom was with me and was helping me through my divorce. I left my husband and Mom took me in and she was being very supportive. Dad was in the hospital and he would never be coming home again. It was his lungs. Smoking was my guess. What an awful way to go. Now

I felt really bad as Mom had been there for me when I needed her the most. I felt a guilt and a moral obligation to stop thinking bad things about my parents. It was the kind of guilt that nibbled away at me.

Let it go, please, Emily. Please, just let it go. Dad was in the hospital a long time and it was awful. When my mother and I made the trip in to visit with him, he was way too sick or out of it to talk and would be reaching in the air for things that were not there or looking off into some distant land. The months had gone by and I'd not had a word from Dad, but sometimes when my sister and brother went in to visit, Dad could talk. Mom would hear this and want to drive in right away to visit. It didn't matter if there was a huge snowstorm. Off we would go, but Dad would have a relapse and not a word would come out of him. Sometimes he would seem to be in so much pain we would get the nurse to give him something.

I caused some upset asking about Dad and this same nurse said there was nothing that they could do. He was sitting up against the wall on his little hospital bed, shaking, and he had goop in his eyes and blood down on his legs. I felt that there was something that they could do, and even said that to this nurse. I was getting mad at her and said to her, "What do you want me to do? Go home, have dinner, and watch TV, knowing that Dad looks so bad?" It would turned out it wasn't that Dad couldn't talk. It was because he was playing some kind of sick game with Mom and I. I believed much later that Dad did this to get more drugs.

I wanted to forgive and I knew I'd said and felt some terrible things about my parents and here she was, my mom, helping me with my divorce. This made no sense to me at all, but nothing made any sense in my life. It never did. All I knew was I was grateful and really I had nowhere else to go until my divorce went through. I'd moved in with her and said, "Listen, why don't we cook dinners every other night. It'd give me some normal feelings and you can rest and watch your

T.V. shows." I thought this was our chance to bond, this didn't last but one dinner.

I was in the kitchen and was going to drain the boiling potato water into the kitchen sink. In walked Mom. I stopped and said, "Careful, Mom. This is boiling. I'm going to drain it."

I lifted up the pot with oven mitts on my hands and headed to the kitchen sink. Instead of moving out of the way, Mom stepped right in front of me. I almost wore boiling water. "Mom!" I said, moving fast to place the pot of boiling water down. "What are you doing? I was heading for the sink."

In that same flat voice, Mom said, "Oh-oh, I don't know." She made a huffing sound, then walked back into the living room. This time, I thought maybe it was her age. I tried not to worry. I was smiling, trying to put on a happy face. I was very glad to have my mother's help at that time and she was being very nice to me, but the strange voice she got … this stuff kept going on. Nothing big on its own, just a tingling feeling or premonition something horrible was about to happen. I felt totally helplessness, unable to do anything to prevent it.

I was also helping Evan and Nancy, as they needed a break at this time from driving Mom to visit with Dad at the hospital. They had been doing this for months now, and it was about a four-hour drive for both of them to get to Mom's house. So I was helping them out. It was a bit of a win-win, so some of my earlier guilt had left about moving in with Mom.

CHAPTER 52: WHO IS THIS WOMAN?

Mom was moving some money around for my divorce lawyer. She was really being quite sweet to me. We have been going out for lunches. I felt maybe things would get better. I must say I really needed her help and she was there. I went with Mom to the bank because Mom had always had trouble with numbers and money, so I thought between the two of us it couldn't hurt. Mom would say, "I can't change ten dollars from a twenty." Her words, not mine. She has always been rather lost when it came to money.

We went to her bank and she sat down in this office and she couldn't find her glasses. "Oh no, here they are." She dropped a paper. There was a silly sort of chatter going on between us. Then she dropped something else and was picking it up. I was thinking, *it's a good thing I am here.* In walked this banker guy. Mom looked up, put on her glasses, and became someone I had never seen before. Looking up at her, I was both started and confused. I coughed or was it choking? Who was this person?

Mom sat right up and addressed him about facts and figures in a voice I had never heard her use. What was this confidence? She wasn't sounding silly like she usually did. She sounded in charge. This banker talked to her like he knew her and she was a genius or something. Quite clearly, Mom and this banker have talked before, and let me tell you, she was having no troubles at all. I listened to this money wizard talking. Who was this? This wasn't my mom. Where did the other person go? You know, the one who couldn't make change, ten dollars from a twenty? What was happening? What's happening? What was going on?

Oh, there it was, that feeling of my life draining out of me. We were doing so well, getting along just fine. I felt like we were getting to know one another, doing lunches, going to yard sales. Her attitude or her demeanour and even her voice weren't the same. Something had completely changed. I was overwhelmed, thinking, *has she been hiding who she really is?* I was in a full on freeze-up unsure of my next move. I had to get out of there. I needed fresh air, so made an excuse so not to have my eyeballs fall out and land on this guy's desk.

I left for outside and leaned up against the building. I couldn't breathe. There was the sound of little birds chirping and cars passing by, but all I could hear was the sound of my own heart beating. The word distorted came to mind. I couldn't think. How many surprises was I going to get? My divorce was coming to a head and boom, Mom turned into a person I'd never seen before.

Thankfully, one of my girlfriends came along who I had not seen in years. She takes one look at me and then takes my picture and said "What has happened to you? You look like you've seen a ghost!" I hugged her and we made plans to get together.

I didn't have a clue what I had just seen. I was thinking, *who's that lady inside the bank? It's not my mother.* My mind was racing and I didn't say anything to my girlfriend. Sure, she looked like my mother but I had never seen this women before in my life. Who was that?

My girlfriend and I planned to get together and I said, "How about tonight?" Out walked Mom and I watched her features for some small sign of which version of herself she was. I was numb. I went home with Mom and got sick. The good news was I could go and visit with my friend that I had not seen in a long while.

In popped a thought. I can't help but remember this after my mom's "bank person flip" something that my uncle said to me about my mom. He said she was always a little different as a child. He was the only family member who had ever said anything about Mom and her strange ways. I wondered what he meant by this. Did he know that Mom was a very troubled person? Once again, I was struggling to understand what had happened to her. *Oh God, please help me. I'm so lost!* I fought back tears. Please, I can't take anymore.

A lifetime full of wondering why and worrying. Trying to tell my girlfriends what had been going on was darn near impossible. *How can I sit down and say some of the things that are happening in my life?* I lived with my mom for just shy of three months, three gut-wrenching months. While my divorce was rapidly turning into a trial, Mom kept playing games and Dad in the hospital also played games, right up until the day he died, which was right before my trial.

I was screwed mentally, just plain old screwed. I couldn't stay with Mom any longer. She was doing these strange things again. Her messing with my head was oh-so-subtle. I wished I could die, but I didn't. I was even more driven to seek answers, but what could I do with this knowledge. There was a familiar weight on my mind. I have questions, so darn many questions. This emotional blow at the bank left me reeling.

My brother and his wife took me in and thank goodness let me stay for free. The trial began. I just couldn't live with Mom anymore and she was much happier that I'd moved out. See, I did have family and I sure thanked goodness for them and their kindness. I had no money but what my mom gave me and here we go, she was being nice to me again. My brother helped me buy a car, but I was feeling so lost. I had a very hard time thinking never mind driving. It got so bad that I had other people read my lawyer stuff and just tell me if I had to reply or not. Once again I was trying to work with a counsellor. She was very nice and told me because I had a trial coming anything

I said to her could be used in court. So again, I couldn't say anything much with her and she just faded out of my life.

Flashbacks. I had heard of these things. I thought this flashback stuff was only about drugs. But this was what I would say had been happening to me most of my life. I found myself drowning in memories that I'd tried so hard to forget.

I was a mess but I was getting a new understanding and it was becoming quite worrisome indeed. There was so much more wrong with my childhood and my parents. When I would I ever know. One thing I know for certain was that I must understand so I could unlock my lock up memory. These things that I was starting to remember were little pieces of a long and disturbing puzzle. It was like I had a need to study them—my parents—to try to understand who or what they were? Was it me or was it you or was it both of us?

Dad died and I went through one ugly trial. My lawyer could see that I was quite lost and visibly shaken. They asked me if there was someone who could be with me for the ending of my trial. I called the only one I felt was out there and could help me: my brother Evan. He came to the last three days of my trial and stayed with me until it was over; it lasted a week. Evan had to get back to work so I phoned my sister Nancy and Barry and they came right up that night and helped me through the next few nights. I was so glad to see them.

Now I had no husband to distract me, and no Dad—he was gone. Now my thinking grew into full on wonder.

I was living alone in a mobile home I'd bought when the trial was over. My son and grandson had come to see my new place. Thankfully, my son was in construction and with his friends they helped me get my new home together even though it was a mess. My son came with my grandson and we formed a closeness. I couldn't have been happier.

I was free now to work through all these things that had haunted me for as long as I could remember. I did a lot of sitting around in a puddle of my own tears. I so really didn't want this to be me. I'd lived in an abusive relationship with my brother and sister, something awful. Lots and lots of tears. Hopelessness sank in, but along came my new neighbours and slowly I began to feel a trust. I started remembering things and they let me slowly talk about these things that I have carried. It got so bad with my mom playing games with me that I would hide at my new friends' homes on days that I just couldn't handle her surprise visits.

CHAPTER 53: LEARNING TO BE AFRAID

I was visiting with my uncle on my mom's side of the family. He was the one who said that there was always something strange about my mother when she was little. He told me another story when he came for a visit and had a coffee, about when Mom was pregnant with me. "Nancy was just a little girl. She would be around three years old. She fell down a big flight of stairs and crashed to the bottom." This uncle said he had just never seen anything like this.

"Nancy fell down a flight of stairs and we all ran over to see if she was okay, but she jumped up quickly, saying, 'I'm okay. I'm okay, Mommy. I'm okay!'"

My uncle said, with a chuckle, "It was strange the way she jumped up, like she was afraid her mom would spank her or something."

Because she was afraid. Very afraid.

What three year old child falls down a flight of stairs and does not cry and does not want their mommy to hold them? Why was this? Why was this burning question eating me alive? WHY? WHY? WHY?

Nancy, at three, was already aware that her mommy was not going to be kind to her.

These things were starting to come together, but some days when Mom was being so nice, I would fall apart with guilt for even thinking these thoughts. After all, no parent was perfect. I was being eaten alive by these secrets that I carried and I just didn't know where to turn.

CHAPTER 54: LEFT BEHIND

My parents entered me in a teen dance competition I was twelve, which I thought was great because now I was going with Dad and Mom. Mom even made me a new dress to wear, blue the colour of my eyes. I was quite happy and nervous because I'd need to remember these dance moves. When the big day arrived, teens came from all over to be in this competition, even from the USA. It was all very exciting and my favourite aunt from my mom's side came with us to watch the dancing. We had danced and went through to the finals. It was a long day, but we didn't make it into the big wins. It was an exhausting time and so very busy.

There were so many people moving around when it was over. I found my aunt. She was happy to see me and asked, "Where is your dad and mom?" I told her that I had not found them yet, so together we started looking for them. Eventually, we just went outside, thinking we would run into each other by the cars. We didn't know where Dad had parked as he'd dropped us off.

So we watched car after car leave until all the cars were all gone. Now the doors to the hall were locked up for the night. The summer sky darkened. My aunt could not believe that my parents had gone home without us, but I was just glad that I was not alone. I wasn't surprised by being left behind, but I was very happy that I wasn't alone.

It got so dark outside my aunt said, "I guess we'd better start to walk home." I didn't know where we were, but it was about a three-hour drive to get there by car. My aunt was so mad. I didn't know how to feel, but somehow I felt safe because my aunt was with me. Dad did finally show up hours later and my aunt said how upset she was, but he really didn't care how she felt and so we rode home in silence.

These are some of the memories that had popped into my head. This was because of the *Home Alone* movie-I had just watched it again. When things happened in my house, I sure wasn't brave like that little kid was.

CHAPTER 55: THE SUMMER EVERYTHING CHANGED

It was now spring and my mobile home was looking pretty good after all my son's help. I was alone and Mom came for one of her surprise visits. I was driving with Mom to the store and picking up the mail, thinking we'd maybe go for lunch. It was nice to get out. I found that I watched everything that my mom would say or do and I had friends that I could talk with and see if I was right. I was still struggling with the facts that I was learning. I didn't fully know if what she was doing was not normal or not. I guess I was conflicted. I would say it was like detective work. I found that I was now studying her and asking her some light questions. Mom's answers were, "I didn't remember that," or "I've remembered it all wrong."

Today, I had no questions. It was a nice day and I was feeling pretty good. Once again, I thought I was going to make it. How hard can having a lunch be? I pulled up and stopped at a stop sign at the end of my street. We were sitting together quietly. Looking up the road, I saw there were no cars coming, so I started into my right-hand turn. Mom reached over and pulled up the emergence brake, bringing the car to an abrupt stop when I was halfway into my turn.

"What? Why did you do that?" I said to Mom, startled.

"I don't know." She tapped her hand up and down on her lap, looking straight ahead and it's that same calm flat voice.

I was puzzled and very confused. Here was that feeling of being off-balance creeping on to my skin. I didn't see it coming and I had no idea why she did this, and she said she had no idea either. It wasn't not over the top earth-shattering, but my mood kept wandering. She had gotten under my skin. Darn it! My mind was on overdrive and I knew that I'd be having a hard time sleeping tonight.

A few days later, I was thinking, *you know what? I can't deal with this anymore.* I was being detached from my body, again that instant feeling of sad and sick and lost. This started me talking to a lady at the hospital. I guess once I found someone who believed me, I figured that maybe there were others. I was at this hospital for a whole different reason, so after my appointment I went to the front desk of the hospital and asked if there was anyone I could talk with as I really needed to talk with someone. I told them I so needed someone who could understand and I could tell my troubles to. They sent me someone right away; she was so very nice. She took me into this room where we both sat down. Words just poured out of me. I starting with Mom pulling up the brake and things rolled out of me. She wasn't the mother I knew; at the bank she'd changed into someone I'd never seen before. My brother and sister had to stay in a corral when they were little and weren't allowed to come into the house to go to the bathroom; they had to go outside in the dirt.

She stopped me in the middle of one sentence about my life and said, "I've heard of this before and you are in danger!" It was the very first time someone could see things from where I was standing, and so fast. Was this the feeling that I had been living with? Was it fear? I talked to her about a lot of things in my life, personal family stuff, but nothing too heavy or so I thought. So you might say the door was opened and I was going to walk right in. It felt good releasing all these deep-down secrets, even if I was still holding back. She got me. She seemed to know what I was talking about. This was a really good feeling.

CHAPTER 56: THAT WAS IT

I started to talk about this with a close friend right after I got back from talking at the hospital. I was really starting to talk and let things about my life fall from my lips. My childhood, these strange flashbacks, and the nightmares—it all came crashing out of me. Things that I had pushed to the back of my mind. I was too scared to talk about all this before, this fear that I'd been living with. Fear. Who knew?

Thank goodness for friends, and I was lucky enough to have some real good friends now. {I thank you from the bottom of my heart. Thank you for listening to me. May God bless you all! You could not know how very important you are to me.}

My past seems to hold more questions than answers. When new memories suddenly came flooding back, my heart would sink to the ground and my stomach would want to heave. I would later find myself with a whole mess of shame and guilt for thinking the way I did. Truthfully, I was stunned that I had friends who would stand by me. I'd always thought I was to broken to have friends. I would get defensive and keep my distance. I was astonished that I could really be liked by other people. I was dying to talk about the things I was remembering, but at the same time I was terrified about what I might learn. It would seem a surprise was at every turn and I had absolutely no idea what would happen next. I always thought that something was wrong with me. Heck, I was told there was something wrong with me. Mom was not lying about that part. There was something about me that was not right.

CHAPTER 57: YOU'RE GOING TO SCARE THE OTHER KIDS

The dentist. I have just recalled a dentist when I was a child. I was about seven or younger. A sick man, this dentist was. I had a bad tooth and it hurt something awful. I had told both my parents about the pain I was in, but they had planned a camping trip in a few days. I can remember sitting in the back seat of our car, heading off for a camping long weekend. It was awful. On this trip back home, Dad and Mom were fighting over getting me into a dentist.

Mom made me a dentist appointment and I met my first dentist. When I started to cry, he put his hands under my chin and slid me up to the top of the dentist chair. You know those round, hard headrests. He got right up into my face and said, "Stop you're crying. You're going to scare the other kids." He was really scary and I was so frightened, breathing between deep sobs.

Then he pulled out the wrong tooth, and told my mom that he couldn't pull out the other tooth because of the swelling. He did the same thing as the first time on my next appointment. Pulled out the wrong tooth, this time a bottom tooth. I was really crying now, plus I still had a painful tooth. It was dad who got mad and told Mom to make sure he pulls out the right tooth this time. It was the third time

I went that he pulled out the tooth that had hurt so much. Mom later took me back to this awful dentist, who pulled out more teeth, until I hit grade 8. That year, Mom had handed me a cheque and said go to the dentist after school. I never went back and threw the cheque into the garbage.

In total, I lost seven adult teeth because of this man, and my sister lost lots of hers. Dentures were the way to go; never a tooth problem again. My poor sister was now very much a fanatic about teeth for her children, and Evan can't get a tooth pulled or any dental work done without being put under at a hospital. Who can blame us? That dentist was an animal.

CHAPTER 58:
A STRANGE QUESTION

I was 58 and I just had to know, but always afraid to ask. Finally, it came out. "Nancy, you know, to this day ..." I paused as it was a strange question to ask after so many years. "I'm not all that sure which day is your birthday. When were you born? I was always afraid to ask."

She was upset right away by this question and laughed. It was a strained and frustrated laugh. I felt instant grief because I knew this deep down hurt feeling very well. She blinked and her eyes darted back and forth. I knew I'd hurt her by bringing this up and instantly I felt sick.

Nancy looked flustered and her voice was angry, uncertain. Nervously, I listened it was an odd and uneasy feeling. Her posture rigid, she said, with strain in her voice, "Do you know when I found out the actual date of my birth?"

I said nothing more and Nancy went on. "I was sixteen before I knew the date of my birth. That's when I saw my birth certificate for the first time. I was going for my driver licence. Oct 20th not the 19th or 21st, but the 20th." She threw her hands up into the air, saying, "I don't care anymore. What's the use?"

I could see how shaken she was and I wondered, frowning, "Did Mom ever give a reason why she couldn't remember the date of your birth?"

Something about her birthday being on a weekday, but they changed it for on a Saturday, which make this even more confusing. There were never any satisfying answers. Nancy paced about for a minute or two. I didn't know what to say. I think I mumbled something like, "Always wondered."

In my mind, I was thinking, *why had Mom taunted Nancy for so long?* A foreboding feeling settled around us. It would be the first time that I knew the date of my sister's birth. All I knew was that it was around the end of October. I would always try to mail her a card around the end of October. Birthdays didn't mean a lot to me, never had. What can you say to something like that?

This was then Nancy added about remembering Evan taking her by the hand to the basement to hide behind the furnace from the bad guys with the tattoos on their arms who were sitting at the kitchen table. Flashback. Yup, my sister has them, just like me. "What?" It was always so unexpected and without warning. It was that feeling that there was something diabolical going on. I felt numb. Evan came into her bedroom, woke her up, and took her by the hand and they quickly and quietly headed for the downstairs. I was shocked. Nancy then said, "I can remember the cold coming off the basement floor. My feet got so cold." My guess was that I wasn't born yet so they were very young.

It's hard to let it sink in. My brain was racing too fast for me to understand. Who were these bad guys and was Dad at the house with Mom or what? I did like I always did. Gor some unknown reason I couldn't ask the questions that I should and it would take me days of this rolling around in my head. I wondered why I couldn't ask questions.

Evan did what he could to protect us. Slowly this would take hold of me but for now I needed to feel nothing. These thoughts were so heavy, sitting on the back of your mind, day after day, year after year. If you've ever held a dark secret, you know that feeling … like maybe someone should know this. My body kind of locked up every time and I didn't know if I wanted to run or cry or scream or just plain old go mad. Nancy was having some kind of flashbacks, too. This somehow gave me relief, a feeling of normalcy because I was not alone on this plant.

I wondered what else Nancy and Evan knew that was not being said and whether I could handle it if and when they should speak. Discovering that this had happened to all of us somehow hurts more, maybe because it has taken me so long to stop hiding and come forward like Nancy tried to do when she was just a little girl. Nancy was so much stronger than I ever was. Whew, putting this down, it became clear. I know that we would never know the whole truth. Those unanswered questions would remain unanswered. The only thing now was to try to understand that this was not our fault.

Why would Mom keep Nancy's birthday a secret? Why did Dad and Mom treat Nancy so badly? It was so cruel to have your little girl crying behind you in such despair, but to do this for 16 years! Who does this and why? Who were these men with the tattoos sitting at our kitchen table?

We had bad parents and never talked about it with each other, but it was important to get it out. I was not looking for any sort of retaliation. all I wanted was someone to explain the truth. Why were we concealing the truth? Was it because of frustration, fear, or was it because I wasn't ready?

I also wondered if my brother and sister agonized over these things too! It came back to when us three were little kids, and Mom not wanting us to like each other. She had told bad stories about each of us so we felt close to her and her alone. Mom made Dad out to be a bad guy and talked about how scared she was of him. Evan always stepped in and was no doubt hurt because of this. He was used to being mom's protector. Nancy held all Mom's secrets, like the mail and what she caught Mom eating when the rest of never knew that there was any ice cream. I was not sure where I fit in but I was thinking I was Mom's favourite victim. Had we three been dealing with the exact same issues all this time? Our parents never consoled us but left us full of fear, shame and guilt, we could never be good enough. We dreamed of being perfect, but being perfect didn't mean anything. I wanted to despise my parents sometimes I guess I did, but I found myself wondering what could have happened in their lives to make them do the things they've done.

I turned to writing. I wrote everything down, poured out every shred of emotion that I felt I could. Like dumping it off my body and my soul. I must admit somethings I removed from this book, because it could hurt other people or are so awful I can't have it in writing. Mom said things in such a way that she knew I would never repeat it and I was so young when she said these things that I wasn't sure just what she was talking about, but strangely her words stayed in my head, spinning around, leaving a large hole in my heart.

I was now realizing that Mom liked to let me know things like her awful secrets because she knew no one would believe me. Everyone knew what a lost and foolish person I was. Mom had said this for years. "There's something wrong with Emily."

I had to do some heavy reading on people with mental disorders. I was reading everything I could on the subject and it was darn scary, especially when it started to fit. Chills ran down my back because things were falling into place. I'd heard stories told about abuse in the past and even sympathize with friends who have said things that had happened to them, but oddly I just didn't realize it was me.

Why was I so blind? What held me from telling the truth? It was eerie and I felt dumbstruck to think of how much time I had spent around my parents. I didn't let my mind go there. I didn't want to suspect them at all. *Please, this has to all be wrong!* I would let myself be dragged down into the depths of the unknown. It was a very lonely place. *I will not think. I will not think. It's paralyzing.* They, my parents never seemed worried or were nervous that one day one of us might start to talk.

I felt lost into a world of wondering what else had been in front of me that I didn't see. It left me looking at things differently. What were the things that are going on in people's lives that we didn't see from the outside? I didn't remember and then suddenly I did, like my life and memory broke free. My life went in this horrible new direction and I felt more lost and hurt than ever. How could this be? How could my parents be so well liked by the outside world?

CHAPTER 59:
THE PUZZLE TAKES SHAPE

It was called divide and conquer. That was the way we were raised, from what I read and later wrote. Knowledge is power, my friends. Whoever said this—wow, and how right they are. Divide and conquer, boy did I understand this now. After writing things down, I could see things more clearly.

If we were fighting with each other, then we would never compare notes and find out all the crap that was going on. Was this why we always had our breakfast in our bedrooms, away from each other? Was this why we did the same thing at Christmas time, staying in our bedrooms, given our stockings until told otherwise. We were kept apart and told things about each other like we were the special ones. Mom had a way of making you feel like you were her favourite and she liked you over the others. Wow, I just didn't know all this stuff.

I still didn't understand why I had remained silent for so long. What was it that kept me from talking? Things started flooding back in flashbacks that were turning into tidal waves. A childhood full of terror and despair! One memory after another. I'd talked with counsellors in school and out of school and as an adult. I'd talked with some of my friends. One girlfriend had been in my life for years. We became friends later in life in my 30s, and she has heard me tell one story or another over the many years. Like my black purse or pulling up the brakes. When the truth came out, even my friend and her husband were shocked to learn what I was learning.

Like I said, when telling one of these stories, and I sounded pretty darn whiney. "Mom went through my purse or she gave us travel sickness pills when we were kids or she gave me a dress or sewing machine that were both no good." It was a huge puzzle and the pieces were very slowly coming into view and taking on a shape. It had been quite a lifelong battle for me to fully understand that my parents were very sick people. They were very broken and somehow I wished I could help, but with Mom, she liked to spin her own stories to make her life more interesting for herself. It was like she had a front row seat to watch all the confusion she caused. One sad memory after another was all slowly coming back me and I felt sick. Dad liked to think of himself with a greatness like no other, but he was bad tempered. Neither my dad nor my mom had been diagnosed that I am aware of. My studying went deeper. I still felt a need to know something that was eating at me, and I was not even sure where to start.

CHAPTER 60: THE MEMORIES JUST DON'T STOP

There were no pictures of us girls. One of my mom's lady friends asked, "Don't you have any daughters?" Mom actually told me this. I had just grown accustomed to her having photos of Evan and not my sister or me.

Mom said, "Yes, two. Why do you ask?"

"There are only pictures of your son. Not any of your girls? Don't you have grandchildren too?"

Isn't this interesting for my sister and myself, I was thinking as she talked. *After all these years growing up we were to give her grandchildren! Someone noticed, someone actually noticed.* I remember I felt an excitement! I was waiting and wondering, *Will something come of this are people going to open their eyes and see.*

Nancy and I had talked later about the lack of any pictures of us in Mom's house, but we knew that it was just the way Mom was. So you couldn't imagine the joy that we felt. It was so good to think that someone might actually be seeing what we had felt our whole lives. It was a wonderful feeling. Hope, I think it was called. Plain and simple, we had our first ray of hope. Someone had noticed! I could just sit down and cry from this relief or jump up and dance about. Finally maybe other people would know some of the horrors that we had gone through. I should say "are going through" because playing head games had not stopped.

    The abuse did not stop just because we grew up. They just found new ways to hurt us. They did a great job of hiding it, too! They resumed normal behaviour as if nothing happened in our home, even as the skeletons from the closet started to pile up. I was surprised at how well versed our parents were in the tactics needed to fool everyone and how well they could play like they were real.

    I know what you've done, I thought, and now I was seeing the real story. *Not what you want everyone to believe, but what has happened. This moment in time, it's you and me, and it's been a long time coming. It's quite horrifying!*

    We grew up in a blunt reality. It was unimaginable and I was so slow to recognize the consequences of this dysfunction. I still loved my parents. They were the only parents I had and I couldn't help but wonder what it was that happened in their lives to make them who they were.

    In the past, whenever I would phone Mom and talk with her, it was always about Evan. She made it sound like they did everything together. Trying to cause a jealousy between us was my guess. And Nancy got the same response from Mom. We've talked, Mom! This all became more of a huge puzzle. Did Dad know Mom was doing these things? Did Evan? Opening up about what was so deeply hidden in my heart brought awareness! Whatever happened to me had a profound effect on the life I lived. Dad and Mom were always there to help me when I fell, but then they kicked me at the same time.

    There had been so many obstacles deliberately put in my way and whole sections of my life were missing, like birthdays. Why was my memory so bad? How could I tell people? I felt it was useless. It was so hard to get the sequence unjumbled! I just didn't understand them at all, but by writing I could see more clearly because it was falling into place.

It was all so darn confusing, these painful experiences. I continually lived and re-lived these challenges in my life with these random memories popping in. It could be something I saw or tasted. It was quite paralyzing and anything that I tried to do became a heavy responsibility; even just driving to the store to buy milk. I'd have to push myself to get out the door; my heart would pound. I have fought this battle alone for way too long. The nightmares that took over most of my life were now less damaging.

CHAPTER 61: STOP!

I did ask Mom to stop doing what she'd been doing. This was after Dad had died, maybe a year or so later, and I made a point to tell her it wasn't funny. "I don't like it when you put me on the spot," I said. She knew what I was talking about. I was quite clear about things. I said, "The only reason I came back to see Dad was to see if he would say he was sorry for the way I was raised. Oh, and stop putting me down or on the spot in front of people. It's not funny."

Her response, in that same flat voice, was, "Oh ... I thought I was good Mom." Then she walked away from me.

I was pretty proud of myself because I felt I had handled myself well. I kept my voice down and stated what I wanted her to stop doing. My mind almost lost it and I almost laughed about her thinking she was a good mom. "Oh well, I have to go now!"

I was not going to follow her ask more questions. That's all I could say. I wanted to give her time to really think about what I had said. I wanted to have a relationship with her now that Dad was gone. I hoped that maybe she would open up and maybe I could learn what it was that made her who she was. There was no way that Mom didn't understand what I had said to her. I walked away and felt good about myself. I felt we should have a better understanding of each other and maybe she would let go of her own nightmares.

It wasn't all bad times. The bustle of activities of growing children and just living day by day acted as a buffer between me and the shadows of my past. Sometimes I even felt normal and unmarked by all that had happened. I didn't have the time to worry. Only the nightmares would bring it all back.

My troubles were not going to go away. Mom was still messing with my mind even though I'd asked her to stop. She stopped by my home unannounced, bringing me one of her baked goodies. It was the way she was talking that made me uncomfortable. Nothing was said about me saying, "Stop it, it's not funny," or about her being a good Mom. I worry but said, "I'll make us a coffee." Again, she picked up this baked goodie that she had brought me and told me to try it. I took it again from her hand and placed it back down on the counter, saying, "I just ate breakfast. I'll eat it later, but thank you." We had our coffee in hand and I walked her outside to my patio and sat down, but Mom was acting stiff. I tried small talk but it was like she was not listening.

Again she said that I should try what she baked. But this time it was her voice that creeped me out. I said that I would later and changed the subject. Mom got up suddenly and she said she had to go, not having drank much of her coffee, and she just leaves. What could this have been about? Walking back into the kitchen, looking at her baked goodie, confused, I threw it out. Why was she trying to make me think that she had poison in it? Did she put something in it? Never again did I eat anything again that my mom had cooked, remembering the words from the lady at the hospital!

For all but a few brief moments, I'd fall silent, trying so hard to block out these memories, but I know that something was still deeply wrong. I felt more in control, so would tell myself there was no need to worry. I wished I knew or have an explanation of the things in my life so that you could understand too. It's exhausting and uncomfortable trying to understand her. This problem was so very complex for me to deal with and made harder because others didn't see it. Why was it that no one could see what's going on? Would anyone believe me if I said, "I think Mom is trying to poison me!"

When I was around her, I couldn't relax! *How would she make me pay for having had this talk with her?* I knew Mom did not like being told what she could do or not do. It was near impossible for me to see myself as a good person as all the negative feedback I received had made me keep my feelings to myself. I found the only time that I was comfortable was when I was agreeing or joking around. I'd always felt like a burden to others, my guess was because I was treated as one for so long. I carried a lot of shame as my family had a hard time loving me because I was and am different. The one question I'd held onto never verbalized. The nightmares I never talked about with any of my family to this very day.

My life was not the one I believed it to be and strangely I was not at all the person I had believed myself to be. I was more sensitive now to the struggles of others' empathy, and I was told I carried a great empathy! My heart hurt when I thought I saw something going on in any way. You didn't go to school to learn empathy. I felt you received it at the end of great struggles. I read this somewhere. A struggle where you go in with your eyes open, hoping that things will go well. If it turns into a struggle to see how very strong you really are, learn from it; you will see and understand other people's struggle. This, I believe, was the gift of empathy.

CHAPTER 62: SOME PEOPLE ARE JUST BORN SLOW...

Mom, again with her unannounced visits, had stopped by. She was carrying this dress that I had owned a long time ago. It was very pretty—white with some silver sparkle to it. I had not seen this dress in a good many years. I said, "Oh, I didn't know you had this dress. I haven't seen this for a long time." It had been washed and ironed and was in very good shape. Mom handed it over to me, saying, "It would make a good wedding dress for you when the time comes." I was quite taken back by this wedding dress thing. I was not even dating and had not for three years. I just laughed and told her I would maybe have to date if that was going to happen.

Then I corner Mom with a question I didn't even know I had to ask. "Do you know what happened to my skull?" It just fell from my lips, right out of the blue. I was not aware that this question had sat burning in my mind. Now that it was said, I waited for an answer. Shocked, that's what I was because I hadn't realized that I wanted to ask this question. *Where had this come from?* I had never in my whole life thought about this but there it was.

Standing uncertainly, I had the sensation of something breathing down my neck. I felt overwhelmed and more nauseous than I was accustomed to when I was anxious. Her reply was nothing. She said nothing at all, like I had never asked this question. I felt nervous apprehension. Why was she so unreadable? She then reached for her purse and headed for the door. Whatever was wrong with me, I knew there would be no escape unless I got this answer!

Mom very smoothly changed the subject as she was leaving. "I hope you like the dress." Why did she paralyze me so, I couldn't say anything and I just let her go. I did what I always did, darn me anyway. I just sat puzzling in my head, stunned, frozen, worried, and looking at this old dress of mine. How did she get it? I was always distracted by my own thoughts. Where did this question come from about my skull? Was there something wrong with my skull?

Mom went back home and I ran for the bathroom and throw up. A few days went by and there was a knocking at my door. It was a lady friend of my mothers, someone I liked very much. She had come for a visit and I made her a coffee. We were sitting at the table and she started to talk about the concerns I had about my skull. I still had not heard a word from my mom about me asking about my skull.

What? Why is she wanting to talk to me about my skull? I was thinking when, just like that she blurted it out. I was blown away.

"You know," she said, "some people are just born- slow. It's not their fault, but it just happens sometimes." She was talking to me very softly, with care and concern.

Mother, my mind was racing. *Oh yes, this stinks of my mother.* I knew this right away and I was getting mad. She had asked this really sweet lady over to help me understand that I was not right. I was not mad at this sweet lady. I cared for her, but a fire started up in my stomach and I could almost hear it burning I was so mad. But I scared myself and put it out fast, having never felt this way before.

This lady friend didn't mean any harm to come to me and I sure knew this. "Your skull is just fine and it's not anyone fault. Sometimes when you're born, these things just happen."

She had no idea how very upset I am. I had known her a long time and my mom knew that I admired her very much. I was thinking, *what better way to hurt me then by using her?* This really stank of my mother, but what it did tell me was that Mom was trying to hide something. I did not blame this nice lady because this was the sort of stuff I had lived with my whole life. My mother's friend had been manipulated by one of the best.

So, Mom definitely has no intention in being honest with me, but I did learn that I was on the right path or why would she have sent this sweet lady over. Something happened to my skull! I wanted very much to cry. I was so hurt and scared. Oh my God, something had happened to my skull! I reached up and felt my skull. I'd always had two evenish ridges that run from front to back. I'd always had them but thought they were normal because they were so evenish.

CHAPTER 63: FEEL MY SKULL

A friend that I had been talking with had come by after this lady left, wanting to know if I was alright. I told her what had been said.

"Let's go," she said. She was mad about this and wanted answers as much as I do, so we drove right over to this retired nurse's home and came in for a strange kind of visit. This would be the very first time someone felt my head, because I'd always known that I have these two even-ish ridges that run from the front of my skull to the back, but were they normal because they were fairly even, so I thought maybe it was just normal. They hid just inside my hair line.

I couldn't hold back any longer. "Can you feel my skull and let me know if it's normal?" I guess somewhere, buried deep in my subconscious, some part of me wanted to know.

She was out of her chair without a word of why and had her hands on my skull. Maybe she could feel my heavy heart. "Well it feels to me that your skull has been broken. It's settled back down a little bit crooked. A hospital would never send you home with your skull like this." Her hands were running over the back part of my skull, and she then added, "My guess is that you have not seen a doctor over this."

I could hear her talking, but it was just so unreal. I guessed I was numb.

She went on, saying, "The way this feels is the sides went flat out to the right and left, but the back top is pushed back. You were hit and hit hard from the front." She then paused and added, "I think that it may have been a 2 by 4 because both sides are so even. That's how it feels to me, but I'm guessing. The back of your skull has the feeling of being pushed back from the impact."

I didn't know how to describe the shape of my skull because my brain pushed the broken parts into a small sort of pyramid-shaped point on the top of my head, with two broken back pieces pushed back by the back of my head. This was how I felt it.

I didn't really remember how I felt at this time. I think I was empty and sad and sick. This nurse sat down and asked me if I ever had any nightmares because that would be part of the head trauma. Yes, I sure did. I told her they were reoccurring nightmares for a good many years. "Walls crushing down on rubber, really tight rubber. I could even hear this and they were awful."

She said, "Yes, I've heard head trauma patients say they heard the sound of rubber crushing or like a balloon under water being squeezed.

"Oh my God, that's the nightmares I've been having for years!" I was absolutely astonished, shocked.

"It's the sound of your brain pushing up your skull. In the hospital, we would induce a coma because the pain would be so unbearable. You would have had seizures, convulsions, and vomiting. What about headaches some ten to fifteen years later?" At first I didn't remember, but in a flash I answered.

"No … not that I remember. Wait … yes I had those too, plus dizzy spells." I was quite horrified, lost in thought now, heart racing. No tears but they were close.

This was a life-threatening accident. I was horrified. *Why was I not taken to emergency?* A lump grew in my throat. *Was this an accident?* I was always told that there was something wrong with me … but to cause it! I still didn't fully understand how this could be. It was so inconceivable. This was not easy to discover, nor do I want this to be me. The shame of blaming my parents for this seemly deliberate attack? This was so scandalous. A chill ran up my spine. *Why was I not cared for and taken to a hospital? How come my nickname was stupid when I was just a little child when they knew how badly I had been hurt?*

Those awful nightmares and all those years, it was the sound of my brain pushing my skull up. The skin didn't break and there was no blood. This was just so awful I can hardly believe it. My parents were well-liked in the community. To the outside world, my mom was this sweet little old lady. Everyone thought she was cute. She couldn't make ten dollars change from a twenty dollar bill. Her words not mine.

My God, my parents are more imposters than I ever could have imagined, evil and cruel. Dad and Mom had been playing with my mind my whole life. I was nothing but spare body parts. Dad also had a very bad and mean temper, which my brother and sister I think know very well. I went back home in shock of what I'd just learned. I was paralyzed.

CHAPTER 64:
I HAD TO KNOW

So the games' afoot and this time I stayed on track. As luck would have it, a chance arose. Nancy told me that Mom would be at their house for a few days. Perfect! I have keys to Mom's house. I had told my neighbour lady friends who I'd caught up to speed on what has been happening. They had been very supportive and kind to me. {Thank you so very much.}

I went into Mom's house. We had not seen each other for some time and her house was so quiet. Standing there in the kitchen, I wasn't sure where to start. I really didn't have a plan because this was happening so fast, but I thought I would look through old photo albums as balloons had been on my mind again lately. Balloons. Why was I thinking about balloons? Was it because of birthday parties? Did we have any? I just didn't remember, except for the ones when Dad and Mom went out for New Years; they would always bring home balloons. It felt creepy doing this, like I was being followed by shadows. I was definitely shaky.

I looked for pictures of birthdays and balloons, anything and everything. I didn't know, but something! I didn't care if it was my birthday party or Evan or Nancy's. I just needed to know, had we had any?

Why couldn't I remember things well? Because of this head injury. So that was what was wrong with me? Something was up about my head. I was still having a hard time believing that I had been hit.

You know those old photo albums? The ones with the black pages and the corners to hold the pictures in? These pictures were black and white and also had the date and year on the bottom. I opened up this one photo album. I was surprised because it had been torn apart and some pictures had been removed, with coloured pictures Scotch-taped in their place. It was awful and obvious. What could Mom be thinking? Why was she doing this? I was left wondering why again, but this time not for long ... because I spied something else.

I saw a plastic grocery bag from one of our local stores tucked in the back on the shelf in Mom's cupboard where the photo albums are kept. *Hmmm, I wonder?* Reaching deep into the back of this shelf, I took this bag out. It felt heavy enough that there was something in it alright. Looking inside, to my surprise there were pictures. Two whole photo pages torn away. Loose black and white pictures were mixed with some coloured pictures. It was in this small pile of pictures that I found in this plastic bag a picture of me, one that she did not want me to see! I found what I was looking for and I couldn't stay in her house any longer. It was just too creepy.

CHAPTER 65: THE PICTURE

This picture was on one of those torn-out pages. I was a baby and the date on this told me that I was 19 months old. I was standing with a very swollen head at a beach. I wondered if anyone ever asked about my very obvious head injury. More questions I might never have an answer for. My age was peculiar for me because I for some reason I thought that I was older when this happened to me, because of the black out in grade three. I thought it would have been around that time but my mind wouldn't accept that my head was broken and I was only a baby. This was so very deep inside. I just didn't fully understand. I could see this picture, but I couldn't see this picture. That old familiar kick in the gut. It was a lot to digest. I got out of my mother's house and drove as fast as possible to my friend's house.

I was empty. In desperation, I showed them this picture of me as a baby. For some unknown reason, I could no longer see that my head was swollen and I found it hard to even look at the picture. I was sure I must have puzzled my friend, but my mind was racing and I was sitting so still. I went back home to my mobile home and wondered, *why did I not see a doctor?* My mind was spinning. *Why was I not taken to a hospital? I was only a baby. Why didn't anyone help me or care for me? Why have I never been told the truth? Did they just lay me*

EMILY KNEW

down, shaking in pain, and wonder if I would live or not? Was this why my sister said she doesn't remember me much as a baby.

CHAPTER 66: SOMETHING INSIDE ME BROKE

Something else happened to me that day, something that I found hard to tell my friends and I didn't for some time. I feared I was broken. In the stillness in my head, I could feel and not quite see, on my left side about knee level, a baby sleeping beside me.

Oh dear Lord, have I gone mad? I couldn't talk about this because it wasn't an easy thing to realize that somehow your mind was broken. Was I insane? Was this the ghost that had been following me my whole life? Flashbacks ... were they all because a baby somewhere deep inside me remembered, had been reaching out for me to find her.

I want to cry and hold her in my arms, rock her back and forth. She was invisible, well sort of. How could I help her? She followed me around for some time and I was not afraid of her. If anything, I felt sorry for this little baby. I could feel her beside me for a long time, and in some ways I knew she was part of me, but for some unknown reason I couldn't quite deal with this.

How could they go to sleep at night as a Dad and Mom, knowing that I, their little baby girl, was in the most pain a person could be in? I kept rolling this around in my head. How long was I down and in excruciating pain? Oh my God, was I hit … and who hit me? Was it Mom or was it Dad? Who could do this sort of thing to a baby? Did anyone ever love me when I was a little? If I turned my head to look directly at the baby beside me, nothing was there. I tried to see her full on but I couldn't. I couldn't talk with her and she never moved or made a sound.

Maybe they didn't take me to see a doctor because it was a criminal offence to beat up a baby. Did my parents worry more about jail time than the fact I could have died? Why did they just leave me for dead? Was it because I was just a girl? My heart was breaking apart. Never had I felt so lost.

CHAPTER 67:
A FLOODING MIND

My hands had always been locked up and I was always trying to stretch them open. Were they locked up because of all the pain? This was something I did when I got stressed—I'd rub my thumb and finger together. Some nights in bed I would put the blanket between my fingers so I wouldn't wake up, knowing that while I was sleeping I was rubbing them together.

Oh God, my sister pulled out her eyebrow hairs when she felt stressed, and my brother slept with his hands up in the air with his fingers in a fist, always ready for a fight. You dared not wake him or he would grab you. What had happened to us?

I didn't understand but now I was thinking about lots of things. I couldn't alter what had already happened and I was trying so hard to understand. My mom, to the outside world, was this sweet little old lady; everyone think she's cute. Dad was known for his great sense of humour.

All those nightmares, all those years of worrying about something being wrong with me. Nightmares that came to drain me … oh those awful nightmares. I had to take hundreds if not thousands of sleeping pills. Why had no one told me the truth? Here my eyes sealed closed and was my little face covered in bruises? Was this why we were given Gravel travel sickness pills, so that we would sleep. This was why Mom talked about the travel sickness pills to put us to sleep, so company wouldn't see the damage done us kids. I do remember Nancy talking about being in the hospital with a concussion. I was way too little to remember how she got there. She also talked once about having German measles and having the oven on and sitting beside it with the door open because she so cold. When Dad and Mom got home they were mad because of the waste of electricity. Nancy did see a doctor because of the measles and I think because she asked so many questions that they dared not ignore her; she just talked too much. The doctor told her later when she was older that she'd had the measles so bad her children would be immune.

Evan had mentioned many years earlier that Dad and Mom should have been jailed for the way he was raised. We were drinking at the time, and I didn't ask him anything about it. For some unknown reason, I was not ready to talk. But it did roll around in my head for years.

I wondered if my brother and sister knew anything about my head injury. I think I was still in shock and I so desperately wanted answers? First I talked with my sister and she said Mom had said something about a baby being dropped, but Nancy was just so little she could barely remember this. If I was dropped from, say, Mom's arms, my skull would have had a good sized bump, but mine was broken. If I was dropped onto something that could do this kind of damage, why not rush me to a hospital? That's it, isn't it? That's the burning question. Why was I not taken to see a doctor? My brother and his wife came to visit me I showed him my baby picture with me and my very swollen head. I was wanting to know if Evan knew anything, but he had no memory of this either. So it still fell on my parents, who must have hit me. This would be why my brother and sister didn't remember me as a baby—because I was kept in my room. Neither my brother nor my sister knew anything about this. How did my parents hide a beaten baby from everyone?

They couldn't have known if I would have had brain damage, and they called me stupid. "Hey, stupid, dinner's ready!" Oh now I had a memory of crunching my body down in my chair and feeling sick when Dad struck Nancy's hand with a fork at the kitchen table. I looked away. It was too much for me to see. Why did Dad stab Nancy—his little girl—in the hand with a fork? Because she didn't say please. We were just little kids. Why would anyone do that? My brother knew that I was talking about our childhood. He had waited a long time for me to finally open up about how things were. Some months later, we were sitting at his home having a beer. I was done dealing with my mother and we had not spoken in over two years.

Evan started to talk. I could feel that strange feeling come over my body and I knew it well. It was something in the voice, almost chilling. Evan told me that when he would go to work as a kid with Dad, Evan always screwed up the coloured wires. Dad called him stupid. I was shocked because I never knew this. It turned out later that one of his schoolteachers found out that he was colour blind. I didn't think I was in school yet. My stomach hurt. This was so unbelievable. So now I knew that Evan and I shared the same nickname: stupid. *Oh God, could it get any worse?*

What came next from Evan left me shocked and devastated. Again, I went numb. Evan started to talk about his right eye, about how he couldn't see from it because of a black hole in the middle and the white floating things. I'd heard Evan talk about this before when he was younger, but Mom had said that he inherited her dad's bad eye. I remember Dad talking about the doctor putting his eyeball on his cheek. So I wondered why Evan was bringing this up again. This time, I asked, "Evan did you ever find out what was wrong with your eye?"

With no hesitation, Evan answered, "I had to many blows to that side of my head." This was pretty unbelievable. This had been happening to all of us. Nancy said that Evan didn't have it easy. They were beating up their little boy. I was a baby, Nancy didn't know her age until sixteen, and Evan was their little boy. I was drained. I'd no idea why it'd taken me so long. I was in my late 50s. I couldn't change the past and I was struggling with understanding of this all. I was lucky to have compassion and support from my sister and brother, plus good friends. The way I understood about Evan and his eye was that he himself tried to hide things about his eye for a very long time. When he had eye tests and the doctor would say, "Now cover the other eye," Evan would change hands but cover the same eye. It wasn't until he got much older that a doctor saw what he did and that's what got things out in the open for him. Evan had talked about his eye when we were younger and I was ashamed that it'd taken me this long to ask, maybe because I feared the truth, or maybe because Mom had covered up those tracks so nicely. I didn't fully understand why my mind was so locked up for such a long time, when my brother and sister would get together try to forget our problems for a while to feel carefree, a momentary relief.

The feeling I had after a night of nightmares was of being sickly empty. Then, just like a leaf on a windy day, my thoughts were gone and I couldn't remember what I was upset about. But this time it was different. This time I had this little baby beside me. I hurt for her. I hurt for her a lot.

I looked back at my lost memories. Lots of hit and miss. Nothing was complete. Maybe this was a blessing? Maybe it was best to not have all these memories. But, sadly, I'd lost a lot of the other happy memories too! I did have happy times throughout my life with Evan and Nancy and their spouses; actually, we'd had some very memorable good times together as the years have gone by, some I remember and some I just didn't. We didn't talk much about how things were when we grew up, but we would laugh about everything else. All three of us had a pretty good sense of humour.

CHAPTER 68: WHAT IS LOVE?

There always seemed to be an unsaid something that floated around us, maybe I was the only one who felt it. Looking back now at my first husband, he helped me get away from my parents and gave me two beautiful children, so it's not his fault at all that we couldn't make it. I'm sorry. I hope you can understand. I had no idea about love.

My second, short, two-year marriage was to the man my mom said I should marry because he would take good care of my two children. He did after all take me and my two children out on dinner dates and he could sing and we went swimming at the pool. After we were married, Mom said to everyone that would listen to her that she had no idea why I'd married him. I'd married him, Mom, because you advised me to. You said he'd get me into a house and help me with my children and that he loved me. She was wrong and I was not very smart. I really couldn't blame him or my mother. I didn't know why he came into my life; at the time he was a breath of fresh air, or so I thought.

My third marriage lasted the longest, with much mixed feeling. He was right about my dad and mom, but he also had no clue on how to help me ... and how could he? I had no clue on how to help me either. I thought I needed someone who could fight monsters and keep my parents away. I did not experience any kind of love growing up; that was what I was aware of now. But his mom was a very strong caring women and I loved her a lot! Husband three seemed to come with lots of mixed emotions. He did keep my parents away, which was something I needed more than love. Now I so needed someone who could help me to understand these surprize awful flashbacks. He had no idea how to help me. It was not his fault. Well, what could I say? It's the past now and I was aware of so much more.

Did any of us kids experience love from our parents? I sat for hours, wondering how did this happened to us. How could I be so unaware? Looking at this baby picture of my swollen head, I couldn't help wonder how my parents could have left me like that as a baby, no matter what happened? I couldn't think about what they might have done if, say, I died and I was thankful I didn't remember being in excruciating pain, not having this memory is a good thing. I wrote this here because this was how my mind was working. Some nights or days for that matter thoughts would just pop in and play with me for hours. I was left feeling off balance. The people who helped me were my friends. They always showed up right when I started to think so deeply and was getting confused. So many wonderful people came into my life helping me with what would seem like simple truths, things that I should have already learned. It's like they were sent to me when I was most distraught inspiring me to go on. They helped to enrich my life and I cherish each and every-one of you. I'd started talking and it was like now I couldn't shut up. I didn't mean talking out loud all the time, but in my mind. Screaming wildly! Help!

I was being heard, and it felt so good to be heard. It was like I could just sit down and cry I was so happy. So now, how could I start to tell these things? More importantly, how would I be heard? The need to be heard was so strong, but I found it hard to put all these things into words. Friends had listened as these little frustrations grew into *wow*. What the heck was going on? I started with the little stories about my life, nothing more than the black purse, the silly stuff, nothing heavy yet. Like a fog lifting off my mind, I was starting to breath. It was really scary at first because I feared being ridiculed, being called stupid or dumb. I knew something was wrong with me, as I still had memory glitches and speech problems, but something was really wrong with my parents. I had known about these strange things for a long time and my parents do things when I was never expecting. Those were times when I really felt alone and lost because no one else was feeling what I was, loneliness would crept into my body and I would wonder what is going on. What my dad and mom were doing was wrong. Now I was watching everyone and growing stronger by the day! It seemed all but impossible to turn my up-side down life right again. Writing it down bit by bit really helped me to understand and see things more clearly. Publishing this came much later on and my publishing team at FriesenPress with their experience and kindness has been invaluable. They worked with me with such care, I'm so very grateful, thank-you so very much.

I found I couldn't relax after learning all of this and so far I couldn't cry or think straight. My skull had been broken. I had a baby beside me that only I know was there, I could feel her but not quite see her and the thing I didn't want to think about was: am I crazy? I did know deep in my heart that she is part of me and I felt sad for her. I was able to tell this to one of my long-time friends. I needed for her to hear about this quiet baby sleeping beside me. I wondered if she would think I was crazy. I watched my friend's face closely. The look on her face was of sadness, which made me sad that I was sharing this sadness with her. I thought I'd mixed sadness and shame somehow together; I was now able to sort this out. My dear friend even said, "I'm so sorry this has happened to you. It breaks my heart." I'm thinking it breaks my heart too.

Was this love? Because she cared so much for me that it hurt? I thought it must be, because I felt the same in the wonderful new life that I was starting to live. It was like I'd been given a second chance in life and I was free. The other day, I had another flashback. They didn't take over my life anymore, I think largely because I'd let so much go with this story. I was aware now and this had made all the difference for me. Awareness! I tried to focus on who I am today and tried to remember that I have a good life, with people who cared about me and I them.

I still had not cried because I didn't think I had any feelings yet. I was in a space where I was very much alone and where I knew no one person could help me with what I was going through or the emptiness I feel inside. This was how I was feeling at this moment in time, right after finding out about my skull. It was a lot to try to understand that you skull was broken and you are a baby. Thinking about the sleeping baby and even writing about the sleeping baby beside me, was pretty darn strange. My wonderful counsellor, who I found online, wrote when I was finely able to write about the baby-beside sleeping "It's your mind trying to work through things." Such a relief, for me.

CHAPTER 69: I HAD A DREAM, YEARS AGO

I pulled my story up on my laptop, a story that I'd been working on for a long time. It came to me by way of a dream about twelve years ago, when I was in my late 40s. Whenever life got hard, I wrote, but it was this dream of mushrooms and a dragonfly that followed me for years. It came to me in place of my nightmares. I only had this dream once and it was like a little movie clip.

What I didn't realize was that after this dream, the nightmares were gone. This took me a few years to realize. The nightmares that had followed me forever sort of fell away.

It was a very vivid dream that made me sit right up in bed in the very dark of night. I wondered if I'd remember it in the morning. I sat up for a while after in bed, just trying to see my hands in the dark. Oh. I did remember it. The next morning I even talked about it. I didn't know why I'd had this strange dream, but I was sure glad I did. This story that I worked on became a joy in my world. It not only helped me with words, but with spelling too. It was my place to go where no one could find me.

The dream was a dragonfly. It came flying up from behind me and I could hear its wings. It was whipped around a spider hanging from a single thread off a tree branch. The dragonfly flew over to a pine mushroom and landed on its head. What was this? It was so beautiful! I wondered about it all the next day, and before I knew what I was doing, I was looking up stuff about mushrooms, then dragonflies. Next, I was writing on any paper I could get my hands on all about mushrooms and dragonflies—things that interested me as I read. I had pieces of paper with stuff written on it, anything that would fit in with what I was writing. I was thinking to myself, *that's what the mushroom would say*. I was compelled, driven with a desire to tell this story.

It took me some time to realize I was writing a children's story, but somehow it was taking shape and I was loving it. I could find myself in the words on each line. I was someone other than me. I had somehow found my place in writing. I had no idea that I would enjoy writing. Remember I had a difficult time with words, plus memory glitches, so why I was writing this was beyond me.

This was what I did after finding out I'd been hurt as a baby. I so desperately needed to feel something, anything other than the hurt feeling of being me.

CHAPTER 70:
A MYSTERY

I had sat down in front of my laptop, oh-so-still in the silence of my empty heart and home. I felt like a lone soul living in a deserted place. For a reason that I didn't understand, I opened up my laptop and went to my story of the dragonfly and mushrooms and started to read it right from the very beginning. This was good because some time had passed from me even looking at it, so it was now fresh for me to read. Reading my story took me away and I was happy to fall into it. The hurt faded a little as I felt I had a purpose. I guess what happened next some might say was extraordinary, but me, I was frozen to that spot in front of my laptop for a very long time and crying, deep from the bottom of my heart sobs.

The first spoken words in this story that came to me in my dreams so many years ago a few pages in are, "My head,… my head. What's happened to my head?" A mushroom was crying "What's happened to my head?" in my mystery novel. *What?* I sat bolt upright. I was shocked at what I had just uncovered. "What happened to my head?" After seeing the retired trauma nurse and hearing about my skull. It was like a guess, a good slap in the face!

My eyes were wide open and a sick feeling came to my stomach. The question that had plagued me my whole life has been in front of me for years. Even when I asked this question of my mother, I had not been thinking anything about my skull. I had never noticed this before when rereading this story, I was shocked. I sobbed so deeply and from the bottom of my soul, I cried loudly. This was why the baby was beside me. My tears had made my whole face wet and I had a hard time seeing; everything was blurry.

I managed to stop crying and blow my noise long enough to reread this mushroom saying, "My head my head, what's happened to my head?" How could this be? It's been in front of me and I didn't notice it before. Why did I have this strange dream and why did my nightmares stop when I had this strange dream? There was some part of me screaming out for me to wake up and understand. The baby? Later, when I could breathe again, I wiped up my nose and eyes and face.

That was when I noticed the symbolism was all through my children's story. A mushroom ... always kept in the dark. Not able to move, trapped and sitting by a tree, feeling as important as a bug. Heroes, heck, many types of heroes all through my story. Had I been looking for a hero to come and save me? In my story, I was sitting by a tree, just like when that stranger had headed for the basement door and I'd backed up and sat for a long time by that tree. "What happened to my head?" Are you kidding me? Even the truths mixed with fiction in my story just like in my life. A coincidence? I didn't know if I believed in coincidences. I was told by a friend of mine that a coincidence was God working undercover. I liked it. I really like the wording of this. Maybe I liked to think that there was a God and that someone out there cared for me. I'd spent far too long trapped with a fear of difference not to hold onto something I guess.

I sat around in a puddle of my own tears for some time. It was hard to acknowledge and accept that your parents couldn't or wouldn't or didn't know how to love you. This story that came to me in a dream. Did my subconscious write it? Should I publish this children's story? Was this the happy ending to my life? It's the something good. It's all coming together. I was aware of who my parents were and that what they had done was not my fault. My hurt feelings somehow now felt more grounded. I did not confront my mother with the picture I had found, and I didn't ever plan to deal with her again. I guess sometimes there really was too much water under the bridge, and so many lies. She was living happily alone with Dad gone, never better.

What had happened had happened and I guess I was who I was. I was okay with it now and I would be okay. Knowledge truly was power. Whoever said this was spot-on. I was my own hero. I had worked my whole life trying to save myself, but something was still at play.

I hurt for my brother and I hurt for my sister. We had all been through so much. The baby beside me was now part of me and I no longer saw her beside me. My counsellor said it was my brain working it all out and she was right. Whew!

Anyone who's going through anything like this must find it in their soul to try to get the help they need. Talk with someone. You must understand that there will always be people who are good at listening and others who will not believe you. Didn't let them hurt you. They are good-hearted people who do not understand. Going to talk with a counsellor or a therapist was the right thing to do. Finding someone to trust was hard, but has helped me a lot.

I sat down to write this true story that you have just read and have changed the names because we have already gone through enough hurt. It was all just so crazy and I wondered how people would understand this, so this was the only way I could think of. Believe me my editor, she has had a handful in helping me put this together. Thank you very much! You've done a super job reaching me and showing your beautiful heart!

Once I wrote it all down, it all started to take shape and make some sort of sense for me as well. I surrendered these private parts of my life, feeling naked and exposed and at peace. These years and years of strange events had really shaken me up, but the damage was long since done. The long-term effects were very real and I was left with lots of unanswered questions. The consequences of my childhood and the many whys had caused me lots agonizing moments of distress. The nightmares that had followed me most of my life left me feeling drained and empty, leaving behind a sadness I could never explain.

My memories were mostly hit and miss. Nothing was complete. Maybe this was a blessing. It could be better not to know everything that had happened in my past. Sadly, however, I lost other memories of my childhood, the good ones. I'd always had a hard time concentrating, but now in my old age I've found most of my friends are starting to have these memory glitches as well. It was the first time in my life I fitted in and felt normal with the friends that I had. I did journaling and took lots of pictures. Most importantly, I smiled a happy smile, pretty much every day now. First aware, then letting go.

Daun, I found you on the internet. You write to me passages from your books once a week. I have written you some of the things in my life and you so kindly answer as best as anyone can with what little I give you. We seem to carry a certain bond of a life gone wrong and I feel a great trust in you. Thank you so much, Daun!

I have trigger points. Things said can send me wild in whatever direction this takes me. I watch myself in horror doing some stuff, but have a hard time controlling myself. This has happened to me a few times. "It felt like the right thing at the time," comes to mind. Nothing like breaking the law, but from what people around me say, it sort of hits me. Decades of conditioning are very hard to undo.

Awareness was the key for me because without this no "letting it go" could ever happen.

EPILOGUE

These words you just read poured out of me. My children's story took me years to develop, but this story of my life flew from my fingertips. It's not only helped me to see, but helped me through the fog. It has been a place to put the things I have carried. I can now let go of my past and place it where it should be: behind me. I've closed a door that I'd opened with the writing of this book. Perhaps someone can take away the veil and find a way to protect the unprotected. It's been quite a struggle and I can only hope in some way me writing this can help someone else learn and grow to understand the non-understandable!

I do not deal with my mother anymore and the tension of dealing with her is gone. I can't see my mother's face, either, because she can somehow get under my skin with just a look or the way she speaks. I did see Mom's face about a year after I broke away from her. We were both heading to get into our cars. I looked down the street and there she was getting into her car. She looked up the street, and our eyes locked. She laughed and climbed into her car and I climbed into mine, holding my breath. She laughed, *why had she laughed? She can't hurt me.* I didn't hear her voice. *I can't let her get inside my head, but of course she did. Not a strong hold, though, nothing like before.*

So, as sad as it is, I no longer have a father or a mother, nor did I ever have parents. I guess my mom was going to take her nightmares to her grave and I can't help but wonder what has happened to her. Dad is long since gone. I'll never be able to ask him any questions.

EMILY KNEW

Mom can no longer hurt me as I know who she is and I stay far away. There will be no apologies or us trying to make amends. I've made a deal with myself not to deal with hurtful people.

I'm doing it! I'm letting go! For the very first time in my life I'm free and starting all over again. My life has turned out quite beautiful and I now live on a farm with a farmer and cows! Love this: me and cows. Lots of land and trees to give me peace. Plus, a wonderful man with a warm heart and a giving soul. Hugs and many snuggles!

The end

and

the beginning!

Printed in Canada